DISCOVERING
ARMADA BRITAIN

DISCOVERING ARMADA BRITAIN

*A journey in search of the sites, relics and remains which tell
the story of the defeat of the Spanish Armada 400 years ago*

Colin Elliott

DAVID & CHARLES
Newton Abbot   London   North Pomfret (Vt)

British Library Cataloguing in Publication Data

Elliott, Colin
　Discovering Armada Britain: a journey in
　search of the sites, relics and remains
　which tell the story of the defeat of the
　Spanish Armada 400 years ago.
　1. Armada 1588 2. Coast——Great Britain
　——Description and travel——1971– 3. Great
　Britain——History, Local 4. Great Britain
　——History——1558–1603
　I. Title
　941.05'5　　DA360

ISBN 0-7153-8959-9

Phototypeset by ABM Typographics Limited, Hull
and printed in Great Britain
by Redwood Burn Ltd, Trowbridge
for David & Charles Publishers plc
Brunel House　Newton Abbot　Devon

Published in the United States of America
by David & Charles Inc
North Pomfret　Vermont 05053　USA

To my wife Liz, who cheerfully made possible yet another of my time-absorbing enthusiasms and never complained (well, hardly ever), this book is lovingly dedicated

CONTENTS

1

STARTING THE ARMADA TRAIL

> Then the Spanish Armada set out to invade us,
> Quite sure if they ever came nigh land,
> They couldn't do less
> Than tuck up Queen Bess
> And take their full swig of the island
> (Oh the poor Queen and the island
> The Dons came to plunder the island)
> But snug in her hive
> The Queen was alive
> And buzz was the world in the island.
>
> *(Old song)*

Through the long saga of English history there is no event better known, or better loved by the English, than the defeat of the Spanish Armada. The date 1588, four hundred years ago, may not spring so readily to mind as 1066, nor 1805, the year of Trafalgar, or 1815, the year of Waterloo. But the fact remains that nothing has impressed itself more deeply into the fabric of English folk history than the Armada.

The reason undoubtedly lies in the remarkably rich crop of legends produced by the single event. These, far more than national pride in humbling the contemporary world's major power, or any appreciation of the political and economic consequences, have been the fixative that have kept the image bright for four centuries. The game of bowls, seen by succeeding generations as the prime example of British sang-froid, the David and Goliath element of the little ships against the great, the beacons blazing across the counties and a glamorous queen addressing her troops with a speech that might have been written for her by Winston Churchill, these, whether true or not, are all part of the popular image of the great Armada.

Perhaps one of the reasons why tales like these were recounted and kept alive by each generation long before there were books and history lessons for all, was that this was not just a naval occasion for the professionals, but a people's war. The common man was called to arms on a scale never seen before and for a brief time the whole nation was tensioned like a bow string. It was not for the last time of course, but the armies of Napoleon and Hitler, though an equal threat and poised to strike, never embarked. The Spanish were on their way in full sight, in cannon shot, of the shore. For the Spanish Armada, the country was at red alert.

There is another reason why the Armada is entitled to a unique place in the record, and which inspired the writing of this book. It was the only great sea battle for which there was a kind of public grandstand view. So this book is a landsman's eye-view of those epic summer days in 1588 — a rather leisurely one at that, because another distinction the Armada has is that of being one of the longest naval engagements.

Imagine for a moment that in the time of the first Queen Elizabeth there had been a South West Coastal Path such as walkers in Britain can now enjoy and that you had decided to take a couple of weeks holiday in July 1588 to walk along it, you could have followed the progress of the battle all the way through Cornwall, Devon, Dorset and Hampshire, because its average rate of progress was two miles an hour. Admittedly the sea distances were in a straight line and your coastal route would be much more meandering, but with a few short cuts and a lift or two from a friendly waggoner you could have made it. As well as stopping for clifftop views of the fleets and sometimes of the fighting, you would have passed through the bustle and excitement, to say nothing of the wrangling and confusion, going on in every creek and port.

The purpose of this book is to recreate an Armada trail through Britain, unfolding the story as it happened, not so much against the backcloth of power politics, military strategy and religious fervour which is the stuff of history books, but as seen by an observer on land. More especially it is an introduction to those places where you may for a moment relive on the spot the events which changed the course of history and cast England firmly for a role among the great powers. It is a trail which will take us all over the British Isles because this is not just a story of the Channel coast. The Armada has left its mark in many places. It will take us to windy headlands where anxious eyes scanned the horizon, to busy ports and to quiet coves which still seem to be sleeping with the memory, to stately homes and to back streets which echoed with the alarms, to London and many places inland. On the way we shall find some of the relics and memorials that remain to be seen and perhaps all that is left of those reputed fabulous treasures supposed to have gone to the bottom on British shores when the mighty invasion fleet was scattered. Four hundred years later the search for Spanish gold goes on, sometimes for the sake of scholarship and sometimes not.

The journey starts at the western tip of Cornwall, progresses along the whole southern coast of England, up the east coast to Scotland and the furthest isles and south again down Ireland's west coast where so many Spanish ships met their doom. Few will want to cover all that ground, at least in one go, but it is hoped this book will be a companion to discovering Armada Britain on holidays or shorter excursions. Where there are opportunities for walks, or other items of interest to see, these have been mentioned. Alternatively you can enjoy this book simply as an armchair traveller. Either way you will not need much imagination to relive the days when the Dons sighted Devon and Drake 'drummed them up the Channel as he drummed them long ago'.

2

WHY IT ALL HAPPENED

You are to understand the object of your expedition which is to recover countries to the Church now oppressed by enemies of the true faith.

(King Philip of Spain to the commander of the Armada)

Before we begin our marathon trail round Britain in search of the Armada it will be as well to remind ourselves what it was all about. It was a religious war, or so it has been labelled. Four hundred years later the daily news reminds us that religious belief can still inflame conflict, or at least offer a convenient front to hide other interests, other motives. So it was when Catholic Philip of Spain sent his mighty force against Protestant Elizabeth of England. On both sides of the Channel were many who sincerely believed they were fighting for the faith, but who knew full well that there were other reasons, political and perhaps above all economic, why the defeat of the other side would be convenient. For a beginning, insofar as anything in history has a clear beginning, we have to go back to that larger than life English monarch, Henry the Eighth.

It is the common currency of popular history that bluff King Hal, notorious for having had six wives, turned England Protestant and caused a major rift in Christendom because he wanted a divorce which the pope, upholding the strong objection of the Roman Church to divorce, would not grant. Henry promptly declared a unilateral ecclesiastical independence, creating the Church of England, which became in time the worldwide Anglican Communion, of which all British monarchs since have been Supreme Governor.

12

In this simplified version of events there is a sparse truth. Henry wanted an end to his marriage all right. He wanted to be rid of Catherine of Aragon, his first wife whom he married in 1509, in order to marry Anne Boleyn, not because he wanted a change of companion, for what absolute monarch ever scrupled to take a mistress or two, but because he badly needed a healthy, legitimate male heir, which Catherine had failed to provide. When Henry petitioned Rome he did so as a faithful son of the church and he fully expected to have his plea granted. There was in fact no great matter of principle involved in releasing him from his vows. In modern times it is a strictly held rule of the Roman Catholic Church, shared indeed by the Anglican and other denominations, that it does not countenance the break up of marriages, but in the sixteenth century when the question of a male heir being produced by a powerful monarch might effect the fate of nations, Rome was pragmatic enough to make exceptions. The marriage of Louis the Twelfth of France had been dissolved on grounds of state convenience and only recently Henry's sister, Queen Margaret of Scotland, had been given a divorce by Pope Clement the Seventh for less weighty reasons. What prevented the Pope obliging Henry was not his sacred duty to uphold the sanctity of the marriage vows, but fear of the most powerful ruler in Europe, Emperor Charles the Fifth of Germany and King of Spain — Catherine of Aragon was his aunt. The pressure he could bring to bear on the Pontiff was tremendous and he would not be likely to remain idle while a member of his family was cast aside by a flamboyant, upstart Welshman.

Many people in England were not too happy about offending the emperor either. They feared an economic backlash in the form of sanctions against the English wool trade, then the main basis of the nation's prosperity and one which had turned the country from a land of feudal barons to one of influential merchants, in other words the emergent middle classes. As for the ordinary people, it may be supposed most of them had no strong feelings on the rift with Rome so long as life went on

13

peacefully. The real problems arose with the landed families who wielded great influence and power in the shires. Most were happy to follow the King, sharing his growing dislike of foreign interference with English affairs, but many vowed they would not abandon their belief in the spiritual authority of Rome, a vow many of the same families have kept to this day. To Tudor England they represented a security risk as we shall see, but others wisely found a solution in Matthew 22: 21, keeping their belief while rendering unto Caesar. In the troubled decades ahead such families served their country loyally in all matters temporal, as their descendants have continued to do.

To put matters technically straight, although we always talk loosely of Henry the Eighth's divorce, he was really asking the pope to declare his marriage invalid, on the grounds that Catherine was the widow of his late brother Arthur and he should never have married her in the first place. All this had little to do with the Reformation, which had been gaining ground in Western Europe since Luther's denunciation of Roman attitudes in 1517, but it naturally lent strength to English supporters of theological revision. Henry himself had no desire for doctrinal change, but he replaced Cardinal Wolsey with Thomas Cranmer as Archbishop of Canterbury and Cranmer it was who became the chief architect of the English Reformation, dying for it at the stake in the next reign. He is also remembered as the mastermind of the incomparable Book of Common Prayer. To the King however he was a compliant prelate prepared to cock a snook at the Pontiff, declare the sovereign a free man and marry him afresh.

Henry's treatment of Catherine was disliked in the country at large, but there was no doubt about the popularity of his next move, the one which has gone down in the history books with capital letters as the Dissolution of the Monasteries. Whatever people thought of the religious questions there was at the time a strong anti-clerical feeling in the country. Wandering monks and friars were regarded as a pest in the towns. Abbeys and monasteries which had been extending in numbers and land ownership ever since the Norman Conquest were seen as privileged seats of power. Allegations against them ranged from corruption and vice to the comparatively innocuous sale of fake holy relics to gullible pilgrims, the start of the tourist trade. In many instances the charges were substantially true and it has been estimated that the religious vocation of the monasteries had deteriorated so much overall that by Henry's time their charitable expenditure was no more than a quarter of what it had been a century or so before. On the other hand many establishments remained good landlords and seats of piety and learning. The heads of some died martyrs' deaths defending them, but the more pliant members of communities were comfortably pensioned off or offered parish posts.

King Henry's motive for the Dissolution was money, which he needed to finance the strong and powerful kingdom which had always been his overwhelming ambition. This has a direct bearing on the Armada story. He used some of the money to build the first real King's ships, or Royal Navy, instead of relying entirely as hitherto on the commandeering of armed merchantmen in time of need. Among them were the *Mary Rose*, which sank before his very eyes during a skirmish with the French in the Solent and is now so dramatically raised from the depths and on view at Portsmouth, and the *Henry Grace à Dieu*, timbers of which are still in the mud beneath Burseldon Bridge in Hampshire. At the same time he ringed the southern shores of England with strong defensive forts, most of which are still standing. It was these preparations of Henry's, mainly intended against the French, which undoubtedly gave the nation under his daughter Elizabeth the confidence it needed to resist so powerful a foe as Spain.

The money came mainly from the rising gentry, rich merchants and speculators to whom the monastic lands and properties were sold off. It has been argued that this was a short-sighted move and that Henry could have done better. To use modern jargon, he 'privatised' the monasteries. If he had 'nationalised' them instead and kept for the Crown all their very considerable rents and incomes while allowing the communities to continue with their work, England might have moved a century ahead of the rest of Europe in wealth and learning. As it was Henry went for the short-term gain and by the time he died in 1547 the national coffers were denuded once again.

Only one son survived to succeed him, the child of third wife Jane Seymour who died giving birth to him at the age of twenty-eight. He succeeded his father as Edward the Sixth, a sickly nine year old who died when he was sixteen, to be followed by Mary, only survivor of the six children Catherine of Aragon had dutifully borne in an effort to produce a male heir. The reign of terror on which Mary embarked in her zeal to reverse all that her father had done and return her country to the Roman fold did at least as much to stiffen English determination to keep out any Vatican backed enemies as all Henry's fortifications.

Coming to the throne at thirty-seven, Mary was deeply embittered by the treatment of her mother. She was also intensely faithful to the Catholic church. Her fanatical hatred of Protestantism inspired her with a divine mission to lead her people back to St Peter's throne, even if it meant burning them, which she did in their hundreds. Mary was an otherwise intelligent woman blinded by her bigotry and never saw that her draconian methods would be counter productive. Nevertheless she nearly achieved what 130 ships of the Spanish fleet and twenty-three years of war later failed to achieve, by marrying the most eligible prince in Europe, Philip of Spain. So it happened that the man who assembled the great Armada to subjugate England, who became the ogre whose name was used to terrify the young and the simple, arrived in the country thirty-four years before in peaceful pomp and pageantry as her titular king.

In the embassy tittle-tattle of Europe it must have seemed but a small step from there to the integration of the troublesome offshore kingdom into the Spanish bloc. Philip was the eldest legitimate son of the Emperor Charles the Fifth, already acting as regent for his father's Spanish possessions which included the rich colonies of South America. His father's well oiled diplomatic machinery had gone into action as soon as the vacuum was seen to exist and Mary was ready to meet the advances more than half way. The English Parliament was alarmed at the idea, but wanted Mary married at almost any price. The idea of a woman on the throne as Queen Regnant seemed ludicrous to them. It took the next monarch to change their attitude about that. Parliament had little power in the sixteenth century and could not stop the match in any case, but it could make conditions and the main one was that Philip should have no constitutional voice in England. Time might have changed that if Mary had been a woman able to handle her country and her husband more wisely, and history would have taken a different course.

It was no fault of Philip's that the marriage only served to drive the two countries further apart. At this time the heir to the Spanish throne was twenty-eight, cultured, charming, as yet moderate in outlook by the standards of his time and not yet oppressed by the weight of responsibility that was later to overcome him. His personal life was a good deal more blameless than that of most men in his position. He was already seasoned in government and diplomacy and obedient to his father's wishes. It was the latter, not the attraction of the bride, that brought him to England. Mary was by now thirty-eight. She doted on her younger husband and longed to bear him a son, but in less than eighteen months he had fled back to Spain, never to return. The fact is that Mary sickened him. It is one of the paradoxes of history that Philip of Spain, the hawk of the Catholic cause, spent his time in England trying in vain to urge moderation on a fanatical queen. Mary was not content that her subjects should repent of their past heresy, but was intent on punishing them for it. The unrepentant, commoners or nobility alike, she tried to eliminate. As much and worse was going on in other countries on the same pretext and that is about all that can be said in mitigation.

17

In September 1555, fourteen months after the wedding and after Mary's latest phantom pregnancy had been discounted, Philip returned to the continent at his father's bidding. The Emperor, at fifty-two, had become a very sick man, prematurely aged by a life of constant war and intrigue to hold together an empire that was always being battered by enemies without or seething with revolt within. He decided to do what no one in his position had ever done before, to abdicate and retire to private life. So Philip became, before he was thirty, King of Spain and all her overseas possessions, overlord of the Netherlands and most of modern Italy. Fortunately he had in these early years an ability to delegate which later deserted him. Not the entire mantle of Charles fell on his son. The title of emperor and ruler of the German territories went to Charles's brother Maximilian, but with the wealth of Mexico and Peru annexed to Spain by the conquistadors, Philip was easily the most powerful man in Europe.

That was not all however. The King of Spain had a right, an unquestionable right in his own eyes, to half of all the new lands in the world yet to be colonised or even discovered, already inhabited or not. After the discovery of America in the fifteenth century and the realisation by Europeans that there might be other and richer lands across the oceans, the Pope of the time had taken it upon himself to allocate the lands of the undiscovered world. Taking a globe he drew a line from pole to pole, through a point in the Cape Verde Islands and declared that all territories west of that should belong to Spain and lands east of it should become Portuguese. Nobody else appeared to protest and indeed at the time it would have seemed a largely academic point to most other countries, since only Spain and Portugal were then seriously in the business of exploration and discovery across the outer space of the oceans. Half a century later it was a different matter altogether and that strange papal adjudication probably lay more than anything else at the heart of the quarrel that launched the Armada. English ambition to share some of that wealth beyond the Atlantic and Spanish anxiety to keep her exclusive right inviolate, was more at the root of things than an obligatory belief in the Real Presence.

In 1558 Mary died, aged forty-two, deserted, lonely and embittered. She had neither seen nor heard from her husband since his return to Spain. As she had produced no heir the crown passed to her half sister, the twenty-eight-year-old Elizabeth, the child Anne Boleyn had borne Henry two years before she was beheaded on charges of adultery and treason. A similar fate was nearly Elizabeth's. She came as near to the block as passing through Traitor's Gate, the entrance to the Tower of London from the Thames which earned its name because so few who entered that way ever left alive. Mary had come close to disposing of her half sister because Elizabeth was suspected, probably quite wrongly, of being implicated in a Protestant rebellion. Fortunately for England she survived to become the most determined, the most enigmatic and many believe the greatest, of all her monarchs.

Despite the dreadful insecurity of her motherless upbringing amid the intrigues of court (though Henry's sixth wife Catherine Parr had been kind to her), Elizabeth harboured no bitterness like Mary. She was as intelligent as any of her contemporaries, speaking Latin, Greek, French, Italian and Spanish and with a sound grasp of politics and economics. She liked to enjoy a full life, dancing, riding and indulging in poetry and music. But her greatest gift was that of being able to touch a chord in people, whether courtiers or common crowd. Elizabeth of England could command personal loyalty, not just the following of power. Men did her bidding even when she was impossible and exasperating, which was often because like nearly all great people she was immensely complex. Her personal life will remain one of the unfathomable mysteries of history, despite Lord Burghley's intimate questioning of the women of the bedchamber to ascertain whether his sovereign had all the normal functions of a woman. All that is certain is that the Virgin Queen liked handsome men around her and enjoyed tales of masculine bravery and derring-do.

The historian A. L. Rowse says of her reign that it 'was and always will be our Golden Age'. Professor Michael Lewis in *The Spanish Armada* puts it even more pithily: 'What a queen!' No man had cause to dislike Elizabeth more earnestly than Pope Sixtus the Fifth in whose eyes she was the heretical, excommunicated, illegitimate daughter of a royal whore with no right to be upon the throne. Yet before this tale is done he had exclaimed: 'She is certainly a great queen. Just look how she governs. She is only a woman, only a ruler of half an island and yet she makes herself feared by Spain, by France, by the Empire, by all'. The Spanish ambassador called her 'the daughter of the devil', but whether that was simply to please his royal master or because he had felt the rough edge of her tongue is not recorded.

The Pope's view of Elizabeth's right to the English throne was certainly one shared by Philip of Spain who, apart from anything he might have hoped for from his marriage to Mary, had some tangled claim to the English succession in his own right. Failing that he thought that the other Mary, the good Catholic exiled Queen of Scots, should be the rightful occupant and at one time he thought of marrying her. That made cousin Mary even more of a risk to Elizabeth than she was already and was why she had to be kept for so many years under house arrest in the care of the Earl of Shrewsbury at Sheffield Manor, with occasional outings to Chatsworth where one of her retainers is buried in nearby Edensor churchyard. Yet, despite the need to guard against Catholic led plots from within and despite her firm consolidation of the legal framework of the Church of England with herself as its head, Queen Elizabeth the First displayed a remarkable religious tolerance, declaring that it was not her intent 'to open a window on men's souls'. So for the first time in decades men knelt to pray in comparative peace of mind.

On the material front she looked to the housekeeping. The royal coffers were empty when she came to the throne, but while she inherited her father's spirit she did not inherit his spendthrift ways. It was her policy not to tax her people more than necessary and she was sparing in asking Parliament to raise money. The Lords and Commoners were not as appreciative as they should have been. When Bluff King Hal went down to Westminster, always with the object of raising more money, it was a bit of a gala occasion, all boys together. They were not so comfortable with their spinster queen, who was reported to lecture them in a shrill hectoring voice. But she kept down spending, paid back her loans and won the respect of Parliament in a way few other monarchs had ever done.

Abroad Elizabeth dabbled in helping revolt against Spanish overlordship in the Netherlands, while Philip retaliated by interfering with her efforts to subdue Ireland. More important than all however, listening after some hesitation to an increasingly influential trade lobby, Elizabeth let her seamen adventure across the oceans in search of wealth and new lands. When it suited her they went with royal approval, royal warrant and sometimes royal financial backing. Not all these ventures were successful, but some returned enormous dividends for their backers. And everywhere the English adventurers went they trod on Spanish toes.

Foremost among them was John Hawkins of Plymouth who in 1562 made his first successful trading voyage to Africa, buying slaves to sell to the Spanish colonists in the West Indies. There was a ready market and the settlers were eager to trade, but even this offended Spanish officialdom, because all trade with the New World was regarded as a Spanish monopoly and trade in slaves was the king's personal one. We all know what happens to prices under a monopoly, so the locals on the spot had good reason to welcome a bit of competition. To avoid reprisals from their own government for breaking the law, they often played out a little charade with the strangers. On the island of Curaçao for instance the governor came down to the harbour and told Hawkins that the people were forbidden to trade, but added that if he 'should threaten and feign to intend to burn the houses of the town or settlement, in order that they might take deposition of witnesses and prove that they were forced to trade with them' they might do business together. Similarly on another occasion at Santa Maria on the South American mainland the population co-operatively retired to the hills while Hawkins occupied the town with a show of force and burned down an old building with mutual agreement, before entering into 'negotiations' for a peaceful settlement.

After this profitable voyage Hawkins sailed on his next two with royal support in the form of a queen's ship added to his fleet, in return for a royal share of the profits. On his third voyage in 1567 he took with him a young kinsman called Francis Drake, whom he placed in command of the 50 ton *Judith*. This trip almost ended in disaster. By now Madrid was thoroughly alerted to the increasing number of foreign incursions into Spanish territory. Philip sent word in 1562 to all his embassies in Europe to keep their ears open for news of planned Atlantic voyages and the governors of American possessions were warned to display more vigilance. The message was taken to heart by the governor of St John de Ulua in Mexico where Hawkins's expedition was badly mauled after an act of what they saw as treachery in the middle of apparently friendly negotiations. Only the two ships commanded by Drake and by Hawkins himself returned home, bringing a handful of survivors from the four hundred who set out. This incident was the curtain raiser to the struggle for power in the New World that kept Britain and Spain in armed conflict over much of the next two centuries. At that point neither nation wanted war. Philip still entertained hopes of a Catholic uprising to bring England to heel, while Elizabeth knew better than her counsellors how ill-fitted her country was for challenging such a foe as Spain.

Relations were not smoothed by expeditions which the ambitious young Drake, now twenty-four, undertook on his own account, during which he attacked Nombre de Dios in Panama and captured mule trains carrying silver across the isthmus. It was on this adventure that he is said to have first seen the Pacific Ocean and prayed to be the first Englishman to sail on it. By the time he returned home he had earned sufficient money and reputation to fulfil the ambition. In 1577 he left in the little *Pelican*, later renamed the *Golden Hind*, in command of a venture whose chief shareholder was the queen herself. Thus he came to sail the Pacific and also became the first Englishman to circumnavigate the world. No doubt more interesting to the investors was that the trip paid a dividend of £47 in the £, a result not achieved without many breaches of Spanish sovereignty.

Around the same time Martin Frobisher was attempting to find the North West Passage to the anticipated gold of China, Walter Raleigh was colonising Virginia and Humphrey Gilbert claiming Newfoundland for England, all of which in Spanish eyes were acts of aggression. When in 1584 news reached Madrid from its Paris embassy of further English designs in America, Philip expelled Elizabeth's ambassador and imposed what we should now call trade sanctions by banning English ships from Spanish ports. Elizabeth retaliated by seizing a handy amount of Philip's bullion which was on its way to pay his army in the Low Countries, the ship in which it was being carried having opportunely put into a Devon port through stress of weather. When Drake sailed again the next year it was not as the instigator of a trading mission in which the queen happened to have shares, but in command of a national fleet of twenty-one ships. He went under a royal commission and took Frobisher as his vice admiral. After a nine-month cruise in which he attacked Vigo in Spain itself, crossed the Atlantic and ravaged Santo Domingo the third biggest city in the Spanish empire, held Cartagena on the Spanish Main to ransom and burnt and plundered in numerous other places, he returned home to unload booty worth £60,000.

In Spain, King Philip was preoccupied with the completion of his vast new granite palace, the Escoril, 3,000ft (915m) up in the hills, 30 miles (48km) north of Madrid. It was dedicated to St Lawrence and the plan was said to represent the gridiron on which the saint had been martyred. Inside it housed not only the royal residences, but a monastery, basilica, mausoleum

23

and art galleries. It was finished in the year open war with England began and became at once the operations room of the conflict, the nerve centre from which the whole empire was controlled.

Considering the speed of transport in the sixteenth century and the length of Spanish lines of communication, it is impossible not to be impressed by the incredible efficiency of Spanish government machinery. Increasingly as the years went by this was in the hands of Philip himself. He was fifty-seven now, married, after having been a widower for the third time, to Anne of Austria. Since leaving his unsatisfactory bride in England he had forcibly annexed Portugal, foiled French attempts to unseat him, fended off the infidel Moors on his southern flank and crushed any incipient heresy at home by rigorous use of the Inquisition. With such preoccupations the English raids on his distant bases might have seemed a mere irritant. Philip had begun to realise however that what began as illicit trading, then developed into audacious raiding, was now becoming a serious long-term threat to his secure hold on the riches of the New World. Other countries such as France were also making incursions into the continent that was exclusively his. Where would it end?

Inextricably bound up with these considerations in Philip's mind was his claim to the English throne by descent from Edward the Third and above all his divine mission as the chief champion of the Counter Reformation. Hopes of a Catholic rising within, centred round the exiled Scottish queen, had faded after the Spanish ambassador had been caught red handed in the Throgmorton plot to assassinate Elizabeth in 1583. Nothing now remained but direct invasion and he had a plan drawn up by his greatest admiral, Alvaro de Bazan, Marquis of Santa Cruz, hero of the decisive victory over the Turks at Lepanto in 1571. But Santa Cruz's plan staggered even the ruler of the richest empire in the world. It called for over 500 first-rate ships, at least as many again smaller vessels, 100,000 men and a budget of 1,500 million gold maravedis.

Philip spent two years going through the schedules with a fine tooth comb and eventually cut the fleet down to less than a quarter of what Santa Cruz required and the manpower to less than a third.

Day after day His Most Catholic Majesty sat in his own spartan quarters amid the splendours of the Escoril, never far from his prie dieu, scrutinizing endless reports, scribbling orders in his own spidery hand. Vessels and supplies were bought or commandeered from every part of his realms and when necessary he bought abroad. England, amazingly, proved a useful source of supply. Official trading might be closed, but the heathens were good smugglers, so he was able to purchase a hundred cannon from a Sussex foundry and arrange nine shiploads of culverins from Bristol. For his victualling he had plentiful supplies of Somerset butter and Cornish pilchards.

These preparations were given greater urgency by the news in February 1587 that Mary Queen of Scots had gone to the scaffold. They were almost complete when they received a severe blow in May the same year by the incident which became part of the Drake legend as the 'singeing of the King of Spain's beard', a phrase believed to have been coined by Francis Bacon. This was the combined-operations commando-style raid on Cadiz in which a large number of Spanish ships being prepared for the invasion of England were destroyed. The successful accomplishment of the military objectives did not stop El Draco, as he was known to the Spaniards, from capturing the Portuguese carrack *San Felipe*, homeward bound and richly laden from the East Indies. This prize alone proved to be worth £114,000. The whole operation put back Spanish preparations for a year.

Just before it happened Philip had another setback to contend with. Santa Cruz died. The king's choice of successor as commander in chief of this great enterprise alighted on the most unfortunate man in the whole saga, the thirty-seven-year-old Don Alonso Perez de Guzman el Bueno, Duke of Medina Sidonia. He was not the most experienced man available.

Indeed he had no sea experience at all, but it was essential to the conventions of the time and especially to Spanish susceptibilities that the leader should be of highest birth. Medina Sidonia came from one of the noblest and richest families in Spain, but he was aware of his own limitations. He wrote to the king: 'From my small experience of the water I know that I am always sea sick. I have no money which I can spare. I owe a million ducats and I have not a real to spend on my outfit. The expedition is on such a scale and of such importance that the person at the head of it ought to understand navigation and sea fighting and I know nothing of either'. Nor can it have inspired confidence that the self-effacing duke had been governor in charge of Cadiz when Drake escaped scot free after his audacious raid. However, when the king turned a deaf ear to his pleas Sidonia picked up the burden with a heavy sense of duty and turned to the task of filling the huge gaps in cordage, gunpowder, men and food needed before the ships could be ready. The monarch involved himself in every detail, even down to drawing up a scale of rations of biscuit and wine for every man. The moral welfare of his fleet was Philip's special concern. A succession of orders from the Escoril forbad any swearing or profane language. Cards and dice were also forbidden and all loose women were to be kept away from the docks.

By May 1588 the 'Enterprise of England', the 'Most Fortunate Fleet', the 'Happy Fleet', all names by which the Armada was known in Spain, was ready and the peace negotiations which had meanwhile been going on in Ostend had reached a final deadlock. Before issuing the order to sail Philip had one other command. He stipulated that every man taking part in that holy crusade should receive the sacrament before he left — and have a certificate to prove it! Even though a regiment of priests was assigned to the various squadrons it must have been quite an undertaking, but eventually all 9,000 seamen and 19,000 soldiers were marched aboard the waiting ships. The grander sort — the officers, noblemen and gentlemen adventurers — followed after a service of dedication in Lisbon

Cathedral presided over by the king's nephew the Cardinal Archduke, conveniently on hand because he had been made Viceroy of Portugal. There we may leave them to begin our Armada trail, picking them up again as they first sight the English coast.

This account of the tangled skein of events which launched the Spanish Armada is of necessity brief and simplified. The subject has given rise to numerous weighty books and many of the principal characters can still arouse fierce partisanship. For those who wish to delve deeper, further reading is suggested in the Bibliography. Just now the clifftops of Cornwall have a more appealing call.

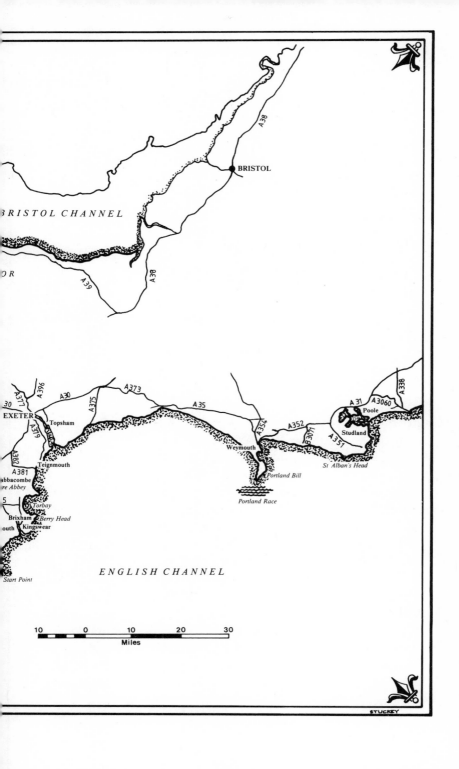

BRISTOL

BRISTOL CHANNEL

A 38

A 38

A 39

O R

A 396

A 3711

30

EXETER

Topsham

A 30

A 375

A 373

A 35

A 354

A 352

A 31

A 3060

A 338

Poole

Studland

B 3071

A 351

St Alban's Head

A 379

A 382

A 381

Teignmouth

abbacombe

re Abbey

5

Torbay

Brixham

Berry Head

outh

Kingswear

Start Point

Weymouth

Portland Bill

Portland Race

ENGLISH CHANNEL

| 10 | 0 | 10 | 20 | 30 |

Miles

STUCKEY

3

THE CORNISH COAST —
ENEMY IN SIGHT

The first land we sight,
It is called the Dodman,
Then Rame Head off Plymouth,
Start, Portland and Wight.

*(Eighteenth-century song 'Spanish Ladies' which recounts the head-
lands passed sailing up the English Channel)*

It would be logical and romantically fitting if the Armada trail
began at Land's End, and there are Cornishmen who stoutly
contend that the Spanish fleet was first sighted there. It might
have been but for another of the long series of misfortunes
which, despite Papal blessing and the prayers offered in 50,000
Spanish churches, bedevilled the luckless sailors.

After the cathedral service the ships had dropped down the
River Tagus at the beginning of May to await a favourable
wind. They had to stay there a fortnight, time which Medina
Sidonia, now styled Captain General of the Ocean, spent com-
posing letters to the king explaining why they ought to delay
their departure. The food was rancid, he complained. The
water was putrid and stank, which wasn't surprising considering
it had been standing in casks since Santa Cruz had ordered it to
be shipped aboard before he died in February. His men were
becoming ill. Still Philip insisted that they must sail with the
first fair wind. Obediently they left the river in mid May, but
then the wind went northerly and instead of heading for the
English Channel they were all swept southward towards the
Mediterranean and it took the main body two weeks to work its

way back to the point where it had started.

By the time the squadrons had reached Finisterre, three days later, a gale was threatening and dysentery was sweeping through the ships' companies, a horrifying but common epidemic in those overcrowded messdecks with their primitive sanitation. The Duke called a council of war and suggested that, at the risk of royal displeasure, they should put into Corunna. The decision was unanimous. Even the experienced fighting sea captains, men like Recalde, Oquendo and Valdez, agreed that they were in no fit state to meet the enemy, exasperated though they had already become with their timid commander. Daily despatches arrived from the palace urging them to make haste, but it took over a month to find fresh food and water and put the ships in shape. Meanwhile several of the smaller ships which had been scattered during the storm, had sighted England. Not knowing the whereabouts of the main squadrons they made for the rendezvous originally appointed for taking up battle formations, which was just south of the Isles of Scilly. When the Armada sailed for the second time this was changed, but had the original plan been kept it would have been possible to stand on Land's End and say that this was where the Armada was first sighted and the alarm given to rouse England.

However, local legend is rarely without foundation. There were thirty-five vessels missing when the main fleet took refuge in Corunna. Those known to have gathered off the Scillies in obedience to their earlier instructions might have been sighted together and mistaken for the main force, though no general alarm was given at the time. It is known that at least one closed the Cornish coast and, finding no warships to oppose her, cruised into Mounts Bay and took a merchantman as prize, so there was certainly news buzzing around Land's End.

Three miles (4.8km) inland stands Carn Brae, at 657ft (200m) the first (or last) prominent hill in Britain. It is also the first of the beacon hills, that simple early warning system that served men in time of danger for centuries. On this journey we shall visit many more of these, but it is worth the half-mile (.8km) walk from the A30 to see this one for its own sake. Carn Brae was a place sacred to the Cornish long before England or Spain were of much account. One of the tumuli that dot its top is where in the seventh century they buried King Gerrenius. The story goes that they bore his body across the bay in a golden boat with silver oars, but no one has yet unearthed them. On midsummer night every year they light the beacon again on Carn Brae and start a chain that runs to the Devon border. It is a tradition revived by the Cornish Society and doesn't commemorate the Armada so much as practices steeped in Celtic lore.

Where the first news was received of the main Armada fleet is, in fact, clearly recorded. At the extreme western tip of Mounts Bay, in which the island of St Michael's Mount stands like a jewel in a crown, is the fishing village of Mousehole (pronounced Mouzle). The houses cling like limpets to the tiny cove which makes its harbour and it is almost Welsh in its tradition of Methodism and male voice choirs. One of its claims to fame is as the home of Dolly Pentreath whose memorial in the churchyard (put there by, of all unlikely people, a nephew of Napoleon) records that she was the last truly Cornish speaking person, having no other language. She died two hundred years after the Armada, though there were bilingual Cornish speakers for long afterwards and today the language is having a sort of intellectual revival.

All this is not so irrelevant to our search for Armada Britain as it may seem. King Philip had always been confident that as soon as his invasion force was seen in the offing every good Catholic Englishman would rise in revolt. In the event, as Philip's biographer Sir Charles Petrie puts it, 'not a dog barked', for he underestimated their patriotism , their loyalty to Elizabeth and the comfortable way in which most of England had settled down to the new worship. But if his hopes stood a chance of being sustained anywhere it would have been in Cornwall where, forty years before, there had been bitter rebellion over the introduction of the new Prayer Book. Intended to be a compromise between extreme opinions it ended up, as such attempts do, by pleasing neither faction, but it was not the theological issues which mainly upset the Cornish. The reason they rose up in arms was because the new Prayer Book was printed only in English, which from now on was to be the compulsory language of the liturgy. It was the beginning of the slow death of their language. Fortunately by the time the Spanish war broke out civil order had returned and the men of Cornwall, still a fiercely independent people who scarcely regarded themselves as English, were content to aid and abet the enemy only to the extent of trading a few illegal boatloads of pilchards.

On a day in July 1588 a Mousehole ship made a hurried return to port. She had set off earlier for France to pick up a cargo of salt, an essential commodity in those days for curing fish and meat. The skipper was hailed by another ship and told that the Spaniards were approaching and that if they valued their lives they should get home as fast as they could; but not wishing to miss a valuable trip the skipper carried on until, halfway across to France, he saw nine great ships on a north-easterly course, every one bearing a huge red cross on its sails. When three of them started to chase him the Mousehole skipper freed his sheets and fled for home where his alarming tale was quickly despatched to Plymouth.

That bit of excitement was quickly over, but it was not the end of Mousehole's role in the Spanish war, mementos of which it can show to this day. The Spaniards ultimately had their revenge on the little port which first gave the alarm. Although the defeat of his Armada was so disastrous Philip never gave up and in the twenty more years the war dragged on he raised several other expeditionary forces against England. In 1595 one of these landed at Mousehole, or Port Enys as it was then known by its Cornish name, and burned the place to the ground. According to tradition the local inhabitants didn't put up much resistance, being petrified by a superstition. The great wizard Merlin had apparently once prophesised that any enemy who landed on the rock which bears his name would burn the town and this is just where the Spaniards landed. You can find Merlin's Rock at the south end of the cove and just beyond it, to prove the matter beyond all doubt, Point Spaniard.

True to the prophecy the raiders razed every house in the place except one, the home of Jenkin Keigwin whom they killed. This later became an inn, the Keigwin Arms, and is still standing, again a private residence and the only house in Mousehole that was there when the local ship sailed home with the first news of the Armada. Embedded in its walls many years ago was found a Spanish cannon ball, which is now on show in the local museum, along with Jenkin Keigwin's sword. On the northern point of the cove stands the famous Penlee lifeboat station, a sufficient memorial to the fact that any loss of bravery induced by Merlin among the local men in 1595 was merely temporary. Half a mile (.8km) inland on the road to Newlyn, in the village of Paul, is the parish church which serves New-lyn. It is one of the highest in the county and a landmark for miles around. This too the raiding Spaniards burned, but bits of the old building remain in the new structure and if you look carefully you can see timbers which still have scorch marks.

We must move eastwards now to catch our first glimpses of the approaching Armada. On the way, a mile (1.6km) to the north of the present road into Helston is Tregonning Hill, 615ft (190m), another of those heights from which the beacons blazed, its message relaying that from Rill Head above Kynance Cove. These sites have little to show now beyond a doubtful bump in the ground, but as they were all chosen for the views they command are all worth a visit. Kynance, on our route down to the end of the Lizard, has the reputation of being the most beautiful cove in all Cornwall and is safeguarded by the National Trust.

Where the Armada first sighted the land it had come to con-quer is known beyond all doubt from the wealth of Spanish records which still exist — Lizard Point, the most southerly spot in Britain. We also know exactly when, but before going on it may be useful to clear up a question about dates which can be a trap for anyone studying these events. There is no dispute about when things happened, but as England was out of step with the rest of Europe on dates at the time different accounts can appear to be conflicting. The reason for this goes back to the same roots as the war itself, the schism with Rome. In 1582 Pope Gregory the Thirteenth had ordained a new calendar. But in the words of the Thirty-nine Articles 'The Bishop of Rome hath no jurisdiction in this Realm', so the English, who have always disliked change anyway, stuck with the old Julian calendar and were ten days behind everybody else. So when land was sighted from the masthead of Medina Sidonia's flag-ship the *San Martin* at four o'clock on a Friday afternoon, it was recorded in the log book as July 29th, while to the watchers on the shore it was July 19th. For the sake of uniformity we shall use the English dating for the rest of this book. Another two hundred years went by before England came into line and the changeover still affects in a small way every British taxpayer. Not only was the old calendar different by ten days, but it began the New Year on Lady Day, March 25th, which is why the Chancellor of the Exchequer still begins the fiscal year on the seemingly odd date of April 5th, that being the ten day jump that had to be made in the eighteenth century to bring in the Gregorian calendar, two hundred years after everybody else.

The Lizard has been for centuries, and still is, the first land-fall for shipping coming eastwards up the English Channel or, as it was called in Tudor times the 'Sleeve'. Lizard means 'the rocky place' and if you look seawards to where the Armada gathered on that Friday afternoon, you see why it gets its name and why Trinity House's most powerful lighthouse with a visibility of 20 miles (32km) stands on it. There was no light there when the Armada came, indeed hardly any round the coasts at all. When the first was proposed thirty years after the Armada it met with fierce local opposition for men still remem-bered the invasion scare of 1588 and said it would be stupid to put up a light which would guide enemies, as well as Continental privateers whose hit and run raids on coastal villages brought constant fear. Another reason they put forward was their traditional 'benefit of shipwreck'. Men who scratched a bare subsistence living on the coast regarded wrecks as a gift from Providence. They may not often have been wreckers, setting false lights to lure ships ashore, but they were said to pray 'not O Lord that there should be any shipwrecks, but if there are Thou mightst send them to our part of the coast'. Nevertheless the local bigwig Sir John Pettigrew got his way and was allowed to erect a coal-burning light which cost him £500 to build and 10s a night to run. Maybe his motives were humane, but early lighthouses were regarded as profitable enterprises and this one didn't raise enough in dues from passing ships to pay and was eventually pulled down. Another was built in 1752 and has functioned ever since, the present tower replacing the original in 1903.

Forty miles (64km) of footpaths wind round the Lizard peninsula. On the west side they connect a string of coves with golden beaches and golden names — Gunwalloe, Poldhu, Polurrian, Mullion and Kynance. On the east side they lead through rugged fishing villages like Cadgwith, Coverack and Porthoustock, whose men must have rushed to the cliff top on July 19th four hundred years ago. Scenically it is a land of contrasts, the flat bare looking plateau inland making a foil for the dramatic visual clash of cliff and sea. The Lizard is best seen in June when it is a riot of wild flowers, one of the last places in England where they flourish with such abundance and variety. The scenic contrasts are even more marked in the context of this search for Armada Britain. Around the fringe stand the sites of warning beacons and, inland, British Telecom's earth station at Goonhilly Down listening to satellites in space. As you drive onto the peninsula from Helston the peace is likely to be shattered by the busy Royal Air Force station at Culdrose, 4 miles (6.4km) from the village of Constantine, at the head of a creek of the lovely Helford River, where they rushed to the church in 1588 because it housed the local armoury.

The Lizard in fact has a unique role in the history of communication in war and peace. In the heyday of square riggers in the nineteenth century when London markets needed urgent news of homeward-bounders bearing China tea or Australian wool, Lloyds set up a signal station on Bass Point, a short distance east of the lighthouse. The ships signalled their information by lamp or flags and the message was taken by horseback to Falmouth, from where it could be telegraphed to London. Only twenty years later, a few yards away on the same stretch of footpath, a young Italian inventor named Marconi set up a hut to experiment with sending an electric signal without wires and succeeded in establishing contact over 15 miles (24km). In 1901, fifteen years later, he crossed the Atlantic and listened in St John's, Newfoundland, while an assistant at Poldhu tapped out the three dots of the Morse letter S. A station was then established at Poldhu, which served world shipping until 1922. Among other momentous messages it received the news that the *Titanic* was sinking. Today on the spot stands a memorial to the man who revolutionised world communications. One other notable communications event on the Lizard was when Britain became linked to Europe by telephone, for at Kidden Point near Kennack Sands they brought ashore the cable link with Spain, hard by the place from which the Armada was first seen.

For all this modern bustle the Lizard remains a peaceful spot, in fact its ancient name was Meneage, meaning the 'monastic place', from the number of monks who sought its solitude. There is nowhere better to discover this and to recapture the feel of it as it was in Armada year, than by following the signs to Church Cove and visiting the church of Landewednack, the southernmost parish in Britain. The church was ancient long before the Armada came. The Normans built its beautifully carved porch, but there had been a place of worship here for four hundred years before then. Its glory is a pulpit carved from a single piece of serpentine, the rock which has made lapidary work the local industry. Polished serpentine souvenirs are sold in the little huddle of shops and cafés which compete to be the furthest south. In this church around the year 1678 was preached the last sermon ever heard in Cornish. A sermon is not part of the office, only an optional extra, so incumbents were free to depart from the English of the Book of Common Prayer. Nevertheless the influences of London, Oxford and Cambridge were being increasingly felt and this was one more step in the demise of the Celtic tongue.

With his fleet now assembled, a floating city displacing 57,868 tons and mounting 2,431 guns, Medina Sidonia was in no hurry to press on, even though there was a favourable wind at his back. He called a council of war to discuss the situation. Nine miles (14km) off the Lizard they rolled in the swell all evening while they debated what to do. The king had clearly laid down the strategy. The Armada was not expected to land its troops at some likely spot and take England by storm, though of course those on shore were not to know that. They prepared for the worst and rumours of expected atrocities were rife, a favourite being that the Armada carried shiploads of halters with which to hang every man between 18 and 70. What Philip wanted his navy to achieve was command of the sea, to hold the Channel long enough for the Duke of Parma with his massive army in the Netherlands to pour across the Straits, just as Napoleon and Adolf Hitler planned in later centuries. The large force of soldiers on the ships, once no longer needed for sea fighting, would then be landed to reinforce Parma's men.

Of course any great commander like Santa Cruz would have used whatever tactics he, on the spot, thought best to accomplish the overall objective, but the poor Duke was not of that calibre. He had formed no plan and now here he was at the English gate with no clear idea where his opponents were lurking. After a long discussion, of which there are many con-flicting reports, a boat was sent away with a despatch to Philip saying that a decision had been reached to proceed cautiously up Channel, but to go no further than the Isle of Wight until they had received word from the Duke of Parma that he was ready. Some of the more experienced squadron commanders had urged a direct attack on Plymouth, reasoning (quite rightly if they had acted quickly) that the English ships would be bottled up there by the south-westerly wind which was blowing in the Spanish favour and they could be destroyed at anchor as Drake had destroyed the Spanish ships at Cadiz. In answer the Duke waved his orders from King Philip which did indeed say that he was to proceed eastward with all speed until he was in a position to liaise with Parma, but the orders did also add 'dealing with any difficulties on the way' and the biggest difficulty on the way was surely the English navy. So on Saturday morning the great crescent formation began its stately eastward procession again, capturing on the way four unfortunate Falmouth fishermen who had little option but to admit what they knew of the ships assembled in Plymouth Sound. We can keep the Armada in sight in imagination as we make a last call on the Lizard at a village on its eastern side.

St Keverne has marked the passage of the centuries by burying the victims of the notorious Manacle Rocks just off its shore. It is an unfortunate community, because instead of being guarded by the saint who gave the place his name, it was cursed by him, apparently for not showing sufficient respect. St Keverne seems to have spent most of his time flinging rocks, which became landmarks about the surrounding countryside, in an argument with a brother saint over a stolen chalice. They were a funny lot these Cornish holy men. The parish church has an Armada chest, the first of a number we shall encounter on these travels and most of which have been discredited by modern experts. The little church guide, which records 1,300 years of continuous worship in the village, puts it no stronger than that it 'is spoken of as the Armada chest and is thought to have come from the wreck of one of the Spanish galleons'. Certainly it doesn't have the design of a sturdy sea chest and no ship of the Armada was wrecked nearby, but it may be rash to argue about it in St Keverne. In any event it is a venerable piece of furniture worth examining for its own sake, and the carved bench ends on the pews are even better.

There are no doubts about our next stop, a dozen miles (20km) inland near the village of Wendron. The Ordnance Survey map marks a hilltop here with the legend 'Beacon Hut'. It is worth the climb for the magnificent sweep of its view, far down the Lizard and the estuary of the Fal and inland stretching across the county in every direction. Local people say that from the top you can see into twelve parishes. It also provides one of the most exciting finds of the Armada trail. For on this silent, deserted spot, 500ft (150m) above sea level, where the alarm was picked up from the lookouts on the coast and repeated to the next up country, is the building which sheltered the Wendron watchmen, probably the only one remaining in England.

The first thing that came into view as I breasted the little patch of rough grazing at the top of the hill was a substantial stone tower which looked ideal for a beacon site, but on closer examination could not have been, having no apparent way to the top, inside or out. As this is one of the old Cornish tin-mining districts it seemed likely that the tower marked the head of a mine shaft, a wrong conclusion as it later transpired. Diverted by the tower I had passed the Armada relic I had come to find, though it, too, is substantial enough. All beacon hills had some kind of structure to shelter the men on watch and to keep supplies of fuel dry. This one has survived because it is in an area sparse of trees but abundant in rock. Its walls are 5ft 9in (1.7m) high, hollowed into the ground to form a chamber 9ft (2.7m) square. The roof consists of one massive slab of granite 10ft long, 8ft wide and 9in thick (3×2.4×.2m). At one side is a doorway 18in (46cm) wide. Driven into the rocks on three sides are iron pins with rings forged in the ends and there is another iron pin on top, fittings which probably secured the cresset or fire-basket.

Although the Ordnance Survey marks the hut* in the Gothic letters it reserves for antiquities, it does not name the hill and as both nearby farms seemed deserted when I went in search of this information, I drove down the road to the tiny hamlet of

* Grid Ref. SW 693 307

40

Litty Wendron. By a stroke of good fortune Mr Charles Collins was chopping wood in his paddock and he not only told me the name of the hill — Manhay Beacon to the locals — but provided a living link with the men who manned it when the Armada came. Mr Collins is eighty and he remembers his grandfather telling him how, when he was a boy, it was still the duty of every parish to see that the beacons were kept ready for use. The threat of Napoleon was not then far behind and although the Admiralty had a more sophisticated form of signalling between London and principal bases like Portsmouth and Plymouth, the ancient emergency system was evidently thought necessary elsewhere and kept in some state of readiness.

Mr Collins was a rich source of local lore. In 1848 a whole generation of his family, five brothers, were caught in one night smuggling in the Helford River after the Customs men had laid a trap. Three were deported and two pressed into the navy, leaving their dependants to cope as best they could. He knew too the history of the granite tower beside the beacon hut. Alongside tin mining another local industry was the production of arsenic. A black rock quarried nearby was fired in a chamber underneath the tower and the arsenic condensed as powder as the fumes rose up the chimney. Young boys were then employed to climb up inside and scrape off the arsenic! It sounded as if the job of child chimney sweep which inspired Charles Kingsley to write *The Water Babies* would have been preferable to this.

As the Armada made its cautious way eastwards it would not have been visible from land because of the deep indent of the coastline, but it is worth a diversion to see the well-preserved castles at Pendennis Point and St Mawes, two of Henry's chain commanding the entrance to the important anchorage we call Falmouth, which in those days was known as Arwenack. It was next clearly in sight off Dodman Point, where it hove to again so that scouting pinnaces could bring news of the English fleet. It was late afternoon on Saturday and tension must have been high for the very first shot of the campaign had just been fired. A 50 ton English bark, the *Golden Hind* (not Drake's famous round-the-world ship, but probably named after her), which had been left to keep watch in the Channel had been fleetingly sighted and fired on by *La Rata*, an 820 ton ship of the Levant squadron, and replied with an impudent cannon shot before slipping under the Spanish lee and crowding on all sail for Plymouth.

The high cliffs of Dodman, rising 373ft (124m) above the sea, with the Spanish ships stretching below as far as the eye could see, must have presented an awe inspiring viewpoint. Today this windy headland, one of the most spetacular on a coastline of spectacular heights, feeds the imagination as well as any place can. It is a National Trust heritage coast, ringed with splendid walks with starting points at Mevagissey or Gorran Haven. The port of Fowey, 10 miles (16km) from Dodman Point and perhaps no more than 3 miles (4.8km) from the nearest Spanish guns, must have held its breath wondering what its small defences could do if a landing was attempted there. It was short at the time of a vital piece of equipment. For over two hundred years Fowey had been the premier port of Cornwall, with a notorious reputation, its freebooting, buccaneering seamen being known the length and breadth of Europe as the 'Fowey Gallants', a name proudly perpetuated by the local yacht club. In the fourteenth century the town sent 47 ships and 770 men to help Edward the Third at the siege of Calais, but when Edward the Fourth in the fifteenth century made peace Fowey ignored the fact and went on waging a private war. The king sent a man down to the town with the message 'I am at peace with my brother of France', to which the Fowey men replied 'We are not' and gave the royal messenger a rough handling into the bargain. As a punishment King Edward sent a force from Dartmouth to confiscate the Fowey Gallants' ships and also, to prevent any future nonsense, to take away the defensive chain stretched across the harbour to bar entry in time of trouble. That chain was still missing when the Armada came, but we shall find a trace of it further along the coast.

By 1588, however, Fowey had redeemed its good name and been given a new fort named St Catherine's, the remains of which can be found on the pleasant walk beside the estuary to Readymoney Cove. Beyond the path continues through the woods and over the gently undulating clifftop to Gribbin Head, another vantage point from which the daunting formation of the Spanish fleet could have been clearly seen. The tall pillar with red and white bands on the Head is a daymark guiding modern Fowey Gallants home. As well as manning the fort, Fowey also did its bit by fitting out one of its own ships, the *Frances* of 140 tons, showing a little more spontanteous public spirit than some places on our route. John Rashleigh took her to join the fleet with sixty local men. In the State Papers preserved in the Public Record Office her name is on the list of twenty-three headed 'Voluntary ships that came into the fleet after the coming of the Spanish forces upon our coast and were paid by Her Majesty for the time they served'. John rests from his efforts in the parish church of St Fimbarrus under an imposing canopied monument, his effigy resplendent in fur-lined gown and ruff. The pulpit here is said to be made from the timbers of a Spanish galleon, though no one has claimed that it was actually an Armada ship. A claim used to be made however for a pair of 'Armada chests' at Lanhydrock House, a National Trust property of no great antiquity 8 miles (13km) inland through Lostwithiel. Unlike the St Keverne chest these do look seaworthy, with locks and bars sufficient for Philip to have trusted his crown jewels to. Experts however have dated the workmanship a century later and of German origin.

Busy port though it is, being the chief outlet for the export of Cornish china clay, Fowey retains in its tumble of steep, narrow streets something of the atmosphere of an Elizabethan seaport. Queen Bess showed her gratitude by giving it the status of a borough with its own mayor. Three hundred years later the mayor was Sir Arthur Quiller-Couch, known throughout the literary world as 'Q', who made the town immortal as Troy in his novels. The house by the waterside to which he escaped in the vacations from being Professor of English Literature at Cambridge, stands by the slipway from which the passenger ferry crosses the river for the next stage of the journey. An alternative crossing for cars is higher up the town and lands at Bodinnick.

Like most of the Tudor coastal defence developments the Fowey river depended on twin forts on opposite banks which could catch intruding ships in their cross-fire. The one on the Polruan side has more left standing than that at Fowey and allows access out onto the rocks beyond, from which there are magnificent views down to Gribbin Head and beyond to the Dodman under whose black cliffs the Spanish fleet lay. The steep climb out of the village leads to the start of a rewarding stretch of cliff walking via the coves of Lantic, Lantivet and Lansallos to the harbours of Polperro and Looe. These were not among the ports ordered by edicts in April 1588 to make ready ships of at least 60 tons burthen to join Drake at Plymouth, so there is no more excitement until we reach the other end of Whitsand Bay and climb Rame Head, the last promontory of Cornwall.

The reader who has followed the trail this far will approach Rame Head along the cliff tops above Whitsand Bay, its long sandy beach kept relatively unfrequented by the steep climb needed to get back. Or the trail can be joined here for the first time by crossing the Hamoaze (the rather odd name given to the estuary of the River Tamar which separates Devon and Cornwall) either by the car ferry to Torpoint or the passenger ferry to Cremyll. The latter is preferable as the landing is at the entrance to the Mount Edgcumbe estates whose parklands always look so green and inviting across the water from the noisy bustle of workaday Plymouth. They looked inviting to the Spanish commander too, or so we are led to believe. The mansion of Mount Edgcumbe was new then, less than nine years old, and Medina Sidonia is supposed to have been so impressed by the sight of it as he sailed by that he declared his intention of asking King Philip to grant it to him as soon as the invasion was over. This was stated by Fuller in his *Worthies of Devon* written a hundred years later and is often quoted, but is rather unlikely as by the time Mount Edgcumbe was in view the opening stages of the battle had begun and the Duke must have had other things on his mind. How impressive it might have looked to him we shall never know, except from old prints, since it was destroyed in an air raid in the Second World War. It has since been rebuilt in the Tudor style and now forms part of a country park which makes an excellent starting point for a walk of half a dozen miles (9.6km) to Rame Head. This follows the shores of Plymouth Sound to the twin villages of Kingsand and Cawsand (as picturesque and uniquely Cornish as any in the county for all their nearness to 'England'), then out to Penlee Point where Rame Head comes into view.

Here we can see for the first time on our journey the English ships which lay in wait. Late on Saturday, July 20th, some of them had anchored under the lee of Rame Head, the Plymouth side as the wind then was. The beacon fire here had already been lit, a fact which we need not doubt because this one had a permanent guardian and his post, which had a dual role, can still be seen. Perched on a hillock on the headland and reached by a flight of stone steep steps is the shell of a medieval chapel, dedicated as churches in high places tend to be, to St Michael. The hermit who lived and prayed here was paid by the burgesses of Plymouth to keep the beacon in readiness. An item in the accounts unearthed by the former City Librarian, Mr. W. Best Harris, records: 'Item, payd unto the whaychman at Rame for kepying of ye bekying and brinying (burning) 3 times — 4 pence'.

This lonely edifice also provided a fine grandstand view of the first clash of the two fleets. Looking seaward a more modern development pinpoints exactly where this was. Rame Head is the nearest point of land to the Eddystone Rocks, 10 miles (16km) distant and easily picked out by the slim pencil outline of the lighthouse. No light was there of course to guide the Armada, but the Spanish pilots would have known the danger well. It was a little over a hundred years later that the Eddystone became the first lighthouse ever to be built on submerged offshore rocks. It has shone almost continuously ever since, though the structure has been rebuilt several times. A few years ago it was automated so no human eyes scan the horizon from its gallery now.

It was at first light on Sunday, July 20th, that the opposing forces first saw each other off the unmarked reef called the Idye Stone in documents of the day. Before the battle begins we will go on to Plymouth to see how the English have been preparing to meet the threat.

4

PLYMOUTH AND THE BIRTH OF A LEGEND

> I protest before God and as my life shall answer for it, that I think there never were in any place in the world worthier ships than these.
>
> *(Lord Howard of Effingham reporting to Sir Francis Walsingham)*

On any short list of the most atmospheric places in Britain Plymouth Hoe must rank near the top. To stand with a child on its crest, where the statue of Drake looks out over the Sound, and point out the historic heritage all round is something every parent should do once. Far more than Armada associations charge the air and even the Pilgrim Fathers are just another group in the long line of ghosts. It is a splendid viewpoint in any event, always made lively by the endless traffic of warships, merchantmen and yachts passing on the Sound. Here is the best place to begin exploring Armada Plymouth, which more than anywhere else in England was embroiled in the long quarrel with Spain and is richest in evidence of it.

The word 'Hoe' simply means a high place and this limestone bluff 110ft (33m) above the sea has always been a natural lookout point. Across the Sound to westward the green parklands of Mount Edgcumbe reach out to Penlee Point, beyond which is Rame Head where we left the Spanish fleet. Eliminate in your mind's eye the massive breakwater which shelters the roadstead from the south-west winds. Though England's peril would have been lessened if it had been there in 1588, it was only built in the early nineteenth century by Sir John Rennie. The massive walls of the Citadel to the left were not there either. This was

47

largely the work of Charles the Second after the restoration and is still the base of the 29th Commando Regiment of the Royal Artillery who drove through its gates on their way to the relief of the Falkland Islands in 1982.

Apart from the modern city at our backs we must also exclude from the picture the naval base at what is now Devonport. That was begun under William of Orange in 1690 and was then known as Plymouth Dock. Naval ships at Plymouth in Elizabethan times were simply berthed and fitted out among the commercial shipping, because in many cases they simply were merchantmen requisitioned 'for the duration' or, as the Royal Navy would say today in the elegant phrase it uses in similar circumstances, 'taken up from trade'. A standing professional navy was quite a recent concept as we have seen and the number of Queen's ships was still very limited for such an emergency as this.

The fitting out took place in Plymouth in what is called the Cattewater, which is actually the mouth of the River Plym, waters now bounded by Sutton Harbour where the fishing vessels unload at the market. It is a short walk from the Hoe, down past the Barbican from which the *Mayflower* sailed and which is one of the oldest parts of Plymouth. The town began here as the tiny fishing hamlet of Sutton, an insignificant outpost of the modern suburb of Plympton with its influential priory, but by the fifteenth century it had built up a flourishing trade with the Continent and was second only to Fowey in the ships and men it provided for the siege of Calais. When the Armada came in sight the stages and slipways around the Barbican, ringed by this time with warehouses and prosperous merchants' houses, had already been buzzing with activity for eighteen months.

Falmouth had been debated at one time as the best deep-water base to defend the western approaches, but in recent years the Plymouth lobby at court had become a strong one. Its mayor, William Hawkins, nearing his seventieth birthday, was now bringing all the drive of the successful entrepreneur he was to the completion of the contract which his brother John

Hawkins in London had put his way. His letter to John preserved in the State records captures the sense of urgency around the Barbican that year:

> The *Hope* and the *Nonpareil* are both graved [had the weeds and barnacles scraped from their bottoms], tallowed [coated with grease] and this tide into the road again; and the *Revenge* now aground [beached ready for the same treatment], I hope she shall likewise also go into the road also to-morrow. We have and do trim one side of every ship by night and the other side by day, so that we end the three great ships in three days this spring [on this spring tide, otherwise another fortnight would have been lost]. The ships sit aground so strongly and are so staunch as if they were made of a single tree.

Then the businessman in old William takes over:

> The doing of it is very chargeable, for that it is done by torchlight and cressets and in an extreme gale of wind, which consumes pitch, tallow and firs abundantly. Our barrel pitch is all spent, three days gone and very scarce to be had here.

William's admiring remarks about the strength of the Queen's ships are revealing. He was no landsman making polite comments, but second in the line of the powerful Hawkins dynasty which had migrated from Tavistock to make themselves and Plymouth prosperous. William was three times mayor, a big shipowner and privateer operator, his name known and feared widely abroad. He knew what he was talking about and wouldn't have been easily impressed. So the English ships that saved the day in 1588 must have been something special and that something was very largely due to his younger brother John.

John Hawkins is really the unsung hero of the Armada, the backroom boy who gave the fighters the technology that made victory possible. He was not a backroom boy by inclination and when the fighting came he was in the thick of it. He too had become a rich man through the slaving expeditions which had so annoyed the King of Spain. Though the third voyage, the one on which he took Drake, was a financial disaster, the first two had returned dividends of 1,000 per cent, so he would probably have been content to carry on organising similar ventures if he had not been called in 1577 to succeed his father-in-law as Treasurer to the Navy Board. He was only thirty at the time, but as a result of his voyages, and more particularly as a result of the mauling he had received at the hands of the Spaniards at San Juan de Ulua, he had experience of their tactics and equipment.

The Navy Board had been set up by Henry the Eighth to equip and maintain the permanent navy, but already it had grown flabby, inefficient and corrupt. John Hawkins purged it. In the process he also 'privatised' the management, with himself as the operating company. His enemies were quick to fling the accusation that he was merely on the make, but he convinced the Queen and her faithful old adviser Lord Burghley that he could provide a finer fleet at a fraction of bills inflated by dockyard rackets that had been coming in for the last seven years. All the evidence is that he kept his word. He also persuaded the Queen that the money he saved should be invested in more ships to increase her strength. Most important of all he changed the design of ships.

What Hawkins perceived was that without a new weapon England would always be inferior to the forces Spain could muster. Up to that time all the fighting nations regarded ships as a floating platform with which sailors could bring soldiers to grips with the enemy. A characteristic of all men o' war was the towering castellated structures at either end where the military took up their positions to fire until they could grapple and board and we still have an echo of this today when we refer to the portion of a ship near the bows as the fo'c'sle, an abbreviation of forecastle. Until a few years ago the Royal Navy also used to cherish a reminder of its counterpart. On modern ships the upper deck aft is the quarterdeck, abbreviated as QD in official communications; but traditionalists as late as the 1940s abbreviated it to AX for aftercastle, and perhaps still do.

The process of change had begun in Henry's time as guns began to improve, and the ill-fated *Mary Rose* was the first warship to have her sides pierced for gunports. Hawkins finished the job by putting guns into ships that were lighter, faster, and much more manoeuvrable. In his ten years as Treasurer of Marine Causes, as his proper title was, he gave England the weapons to meet the lumbering leviathans which had so far given Spain mastery of the seas. A. L. Rowse has compared the Hawkins ships to the Spitfires and Hurricanes of the Second World War, in that they saved the day against fantastic odds. More than that, they changed the face of naval warfare for ever.

Such ships would have been useless without men of the right calibre to command them. Elizabethan England abounded in such men, but the one who dominates this story is Francis Drake. The island in Plymouth Sound which bears his name was already full of associations for him in Armada year, though it was then and for many years afterwards called St Nicholas Island after the patron saint of seafarers. To this island the Drake family had to flee and remain in hiding, in straitened financial circumstances, when Francis was a small boy. Beside it he dropped anchor when he returned a millionaire from his voyage round the world thirty years later. When the Armada was over the city fathers wanted to fortify the island as a strong defensive position and make Drake permanent governor. In subsequent years the armed forces put it to various uses, but it was not until the eighteenth century that the change of name was suggested to honour the immortal memory. It is said to have been the idea of a descendant accused of wanting to bask in the reflected glory to improve his political chances. Today Drake's Island enjoys a peaceful use as an outdoor adventure training centre. In summer it is possible to visit it on one of the frequent boat trips that run from the Barbican and to wander round its 6 acres (2.4ha).

Drake was born around 1539 at a farm near Tavistock, into a family which was well connected but not well off. His father Edmund was a Protestant extremist who was hounded by a band of equally extreme Catholics during the religious upheavals of

1547, which was when he took refuge with his family on St Nicholas Island. Later he got a job as a kind of lay reader to ships on the River Medway in Kent where the family lived in an old hulk. Francis was apprenticed to a shipmaster plying the North Sea and there learned his trade. He inherited his father's strong religious faith, but not his puritanical outlook. He enjoyed the fruits of his success and paraded them flamboyantly. Courtiers in London regarded him as an upstart with a flaring temper and a too sharp tongue. The wiser ones recognised him nevertheless as the best man at the job the country had.

One thing Drake never was, though many writers have called him one, was a pirate. He had been a privateer, which is distinctly different. Whereas a pirate was a mere robber on the high seas who would plunder any ship he could take by superior force, a privateer was legally commissioned by his own sovereign to attack and capture only ships of the country's enemies, including the merchant and coastal vessels which often presented easy targets. There could be high profits, but also high risks, and the Crown took a hefty share of the proceeds. This system of augmenting naval strength by issuing privately owned ships with 'letters of marque and reprisal', as these commissions were known, was still being widely used during the Napoleonic wars and not until 1856 was it ended by international agreement at the Convention of Paris. By the nineteenth century the rules of engagement for privateers were closely defined. They were a good deal looser in Elizabethan times and Drake undoubtedly overstepped the mark not infrequently.

Drake was not a naval officer either. There were few of them permanently employed in Elizabethan times. To find a modern parallel for his role in the Armada we should have to call him a naval reservist. For months he had been fitting out the Western Squadron — a fleet of thirty-four requisitioned merchantmen, in addition to several of the Queen's ships sent round from London — which he had been ordered to command, but for all old William Hawkin's efforts it did not always go smoothly. Some of the chaos that reigned in Plymouth during those months can be imagined by walking the narrow, twisting Elizabethan streets which still exist behind the Barbican. The holidaymakers and tourists make them seem busy today, but this is nothing compared to the jostling and shouting which once took place as carts and men and laden beasts passed to and fro to the waterfront.

This hillside stretching behind the Barbican, to the point where St Andrew's Church stands, was most of the town of Plymouth then. The modern city centre extending beyond the dual carriageway was fields and wasteland. The Old Town as it is now called was home to 2,000 people and exactly that number of seamen had arrived to serve in Drake's ships. Then the Queen, ever mindful of the expense, ordered that half of them should be paid off when things looked hopeful for the peace negotiations. In May they were reinstated and joined by 9,000 more and then 1,000 troops were billeted on the town. Food and shelter had to be found for them all. Plymouth must have been packed like a tube train in the rush hour! It is not surprising that there was not enough food, then or later. The men who defeated the Spaniards did it on empty stomachs and a ration of rotten beer, as we know from the letter which Lord Howard had to write to Secretary of State Walsingham in the middle of the Armada preparations: 'I know not which way to deal with the mariners to make them rest contented with sour beer, for nothing doth displease them more'. Not even a Nelson or a Mountbatten could have made their sailors rest contented with sour beer.

Disease added to the problems. The *Elizabeth Jonas*, 900 tons and third biggest ship of the regular navy, arrived in Plymouth in May and within a month 200 of her complement of 500 were dead, probably from typhus. The present waterfront of quays and jetties was then mainly shelving beaches and here the unfortunate ship was run ashore, stripped down to the ballast and fumigated by burning fires of wet broom between her decks.

With his fortune Francis Drake had lately acquired a grand country mansion, but it was 10 miles (16km) from the city, not exactly commuting distance in those days. But he had a town house which was probably his headquarters in the summer of 1588. It was at the top of Looe Street in another part of Old Town and although the building no longer stands a plaque adorns the shop which occupies the site and the owners have named their business Drake Stamps. Many pilgrims visit it and ask to look inside, even though the present structure is entirely modern and part of a block unromantically called Corporation Buildings. They are always welcomed, though unfortunately for the proprietors not too many of the visitors are also philatelists. Most of the old Looe Street was pulled down in the 1930s in the interests of development, but a number of Elizabethan houses have survived on the opposite side to Drake's house and have been recently renovated, so that only the cars parked bumper to bumper prevent one getting an idea of what it used to look like. Happily there are also close at hand two splendidly restored houses of the same period which are open to the public. One, 32 New Street, is furnished and gives a good impression of the style in which men like Drake and Hawkins lived in Plymouth. The other is the impressive Merchants House now used as a museum.

New Street was 'new' just four years before the Armada, a development of commodious warehouses with comfortable residences adjacent for their owners, bought when trade was booming. A plaque records its builder, John Sparke, a former mayor and friend of Drake's. With the press of men and stores making their way to the quays in Armada year they must have blessed him, because before there had only been a muddy track. Several other buildings in the street bear evidence of their period. Look up and see the projecting beams and pulleys that may have been used to lower stores to victual England's Armada ships.

A passage off New Street leads into a quiet little oasis which is one of the most charming spots on the Armada trail, a perfectly reconstructed Elizabethan garden with formal green hedges, low stone walls and an archway with a carved lintel depicting a ship of the period. Drake in all probability had a garden like this attached to his Looe Street house. Perhaps he cooled off his anger in it during the frustrating months of waiting when the orders from London were all stop and start, and perhaps it was where he bid farewell to his second wife Elizabeth Sydenham when he set sail at last.

As the smoke rose from the beacons on the Cornish shore and tension mounted, attention would have been concentrated on the Hoe where excited crowds must have gathered. Old William Hawkins would not have joined them, though his work with the ships was now done. As mayor his post of duty in emergency was clearly laid down. He had to take command of the town's defences in the older pre-Citadel fort known as the Castle Quadrate. His footsteps can be traced to all that remains of it, a short section of wall and a fragment of turret halfway up the short incline that leads from the Barbican to the Hoe. It flanks a pleasant garden with seats which looks out over the harbour and which is kept locked because it was given by Lady Astor for the exclusive use of the retired fishermen of Plymouth. Nancy Astor was the millionaire's wife who became the first woman to take her seat in the House of Commons. She was the darling of the Plymouth voters who returned her at every election from 1919 to 1945 when she retired. This forceful character would have been quite at home with the thrusting Elizabethan sea dogs of her constituency.

Legend, which seems to have the backing of common sense, puts the English admirals on the Hoe when the first positive news of the Armada's position and disposition was received. Drake was not at their head. English convention, just as much as Spanish, required noble blood in that position and the choice was Lord Howard of Effingham. Drake's appointment would have aroused too many jealousies in any event. The naval historian Michael Lewis described Howard as 'a fine Christian gentleman, a leader wise and talented, respected and loved' and he certainly handled what often looked like being an explosive situation with wonderful tact.

There had been doubts whether the prickly Drake, whose track record clearly marked him out as the best sea fighter the country had, would agree to serve under anyone else. Howard had the sense to respect and listen to Drake and an engaging little ceremony took place on the waters of Plymouth Sound when the Lord High Admiral arrived in his flagship the *Ark Royal*. Drake, who had so far commanded everything in the west, sailed out to meet him, lowered his senior flag officer's pennant and sent it across to Howard in a gesture of recognition of his authority, while Howard sent in return a vice-admiral's flag for Drake. Conscious sighs of official relief are evident from a letter Howard wrote to Walsingham: 'I must not omit to let you know how lovingly and kindly Sir Francis Drake beareth himself; and also how dutifully to Her Majesty's service and unto me, being in the place where I am in; which pray you he may receive thanks for by some private letter from you'.

It was however to Drake that the vital message of the Armada's approach came, because the man who brought it, Captain Thomas Flemying of the *Golden Hind*, was part of Drake's squadron and naturally reported to his own immediate superior. But whether that was really while the leaders were playing bowls and whether Drake really responded to the news by saying 'there is time to finish the game of bowls and beat the Spaniards afterwards' needs examining. Modern historians are a more sceptical race than their predecessors and many discount the tradition on the grounds that nothing appeared in print until 1624 and that it was unlikely to have happened when every minute must have been vital. The first seems a shaky reason for abandoning one of history's more colourful stories, bearing in mind that this was not the age of mass communication, that newspapers were unknown and books a rarity. People in any period recall important memories in old age, not while they are young and busy. The first printed reference to the game of bowls thirty-six years later was sufficiently well within living memory for it to have been written from first-hand testimony.

For an opinion on whether in the circumstances it would have been a practical likelihood I retraced my steps across the Hamoaze to Cawsand to talk to Crispin Gill, who has spent a lifetime studying and writing about Plymouth and its famous sons. His house is, suitably, an old garrison commander's quarters, his study windows overlooking the waters of the Sound whose history he knows so well. There was no doubt in his mind:

> Everything about the legend fits the facts. We know that bowls was a Plymouth game. There is a mention of it in town records four years before the Armada and a suggestion that it was discouraged by the authorities. It probably wasn't like the game of bowls we know today, more like skittles or ten pin bowling and played with cheese-shaped leather objects they called tyles. It is also fully in keeping with what we know about Drake's character, his bravado, his ability to joke in the face of danger and his love of showmanship. He was also, don't forget, a great seaman who knew his home waters intimately. It was three o'clock on the Friday afternoon that he received the message. The ships were all ready, moored in the Cattewater, but bottled up there by the south-west wind that was giving the Spaniards a fair passage up Channel. It was a worrying situation, fraught with potential disaster, because they would have been sitting targets to a bold Spanish attack. The only way to get those ships into action was to warp them out, a long and laborious process that could only be done in that unfavourable wind with the help of an ebb tide. By my calculations high water at Plymouth that day was at 10.30 pm, but Drake knew when he heard the news that there was only the last and weakest hour of the ebb left and therefore another six hours to wait before anything could be done.
>
> You can be certain that all the orders had already been given. There were several thousand seamen standing by to haul those ships out the minute the word was given. As there was no more he could usefully do for now, Drake sensed that a display of coolness and a laugh at the enemy's expense was a sure way to boost morale. The circumstances certainly made the gesture feasible and it was typical of Drake.

So, reassured that the game of bowls did happen, where did it happen? Almost certainly not where the modern bowling green stands on the Hoe. Some local researchers favour the ABC cinema at the foot of the landward slope of the Hoe as there is an old reference to bowls being played on that site. Others think in one of the private gardens, as it is known the gentry were encouraged to restrict play to their homes so as not to set a bad example. But did it have to be a formal game at all? My own feeling, quite without supporting evidence, is that it was more likely to have been a scratch game, perhaps played with half a dozen cannon balls, say from a demi-culverin at 9lb (4kg) weight or with handier 4lb (1.8kg) minion shot. What more natural way to relieve the tension of the waiting hours, just as any group of Frenchmen with time to kill produce *boules*. As for the place, Crispin Gill favours the tradition of the Hoe since it would be more sensible for the officers to gather where they had a good lookout. If so the site of the legendary game has probably disappeared for in those days the Hoe, used for sheep grazing, was much more extensive. In the intervening centuries much of it has been eaten away by limestone quarrying of the cliffs.

Fittingly the Hoe is crowned now by the pugnacious memorial statue of Drake, but it took the city and the nation a long time to get round to it. A descendant, Lady Elliott Drake, unveiled it in 1884, but it wasn't quite what was planned. Plymouth's memorial is only a copy of the one in the square at Tavistock by the sculptor Boehm. The Duke of Bedford who commissioned the original, gave permission for a cheaper copy to be made for the Hoe after Plymouth's appeal fund for their own design had failed to reach its target. The hero shares the site today with the simple modern naval war memorial and an excessively fussy Victorian monument erected to mark the three-hundredth anniversary of the Armada.

When high water arrived on Friday, July 19th, the night air over the town must have been loud with the shout of orders, the shrill of boatswains' calls, the rattle of ropes through blocks as every boat was lowered and the creak of oars as they pulled the ships clear into open water where they could hoist sail with sea room to beat out against the south-west breeze. The work went on all night — gruelling work for men who had been ordered to share four men's rations between six, to say nothing of sour beer! And all for ten shillings a month. Nevertheless over sixty-five of the biggest ships cleared the Sound and by midday Saturday the main force under Howard was abeam of the Eddystone, sailing right across the bows of the approaching enemy. There they caught their first sight of the great Armada, but not for long because English summers were as unreliable then as now and a mist came swirling up the Channel to block out the view.

It would have been blotted out as well to the watchers on Rame Head, but they would have seen what the puzzled Spaniards caught only a fleeting glimpse of — another squadron of eleven English ships using local knowledge supplied by the Plymouth officers slipping westwards close in shore, on the back eddy that runs there when the flood tide is at its peak further out to sea. So on Sunday morning at first light the Armada had been passed on both sides and found the English astern. Medina Sidonia's inaction had lost them the weather gauge, the windward position so vital throughout the age of fighting sail.

From our position on Rame Head we might now have seen, at least with a good telescope, a strange little ceremony take place. An air of medieval chivalry still clung to warfare in the sixteenth century and certain courtesies had to be observed before you could blow a chap's head off. Lord Admiral Howard (on £3 a day which was twice Drake's pay) sent off a single 80 ton pinnace, nicely named the *Disdain*, to issue a challenge to his opposite number. Sailing all alone up to the solid wall of galleons the *Disdain* discharged a single tiny shot in the direction of the Spanish flagship. The like being received in reply honour was now satisfied and battle could commence.

One dramatic moment of the engagement was certainly visible from the vantage points on land. Almost as soon as the fighting had begun a great explosion rent the 950 ton *San Salvador* of Miguel de Oquendo's squadron, which ship carried the paymaster general and a large proportion of the Armada's treasury, some of which was intended to fund any English Catholic gentry who might rise in Spain's support. This explosion was not the result of English gunnery but was rumoured to be due to the revenge of a foreign seaman who had been whipped by the captain and who threw a lighted match into a barrel of gunpowder before jumping overboard. The explosion blew the stern out of the ship and killed two hundred men. It may equally well have been an accident of the type common enough in the early days of gunpowder in ships.

That was the highlight of the fireworks for Plymouth area spectators. After a brisk exchange of fire Howard held his ships back. With the advantage of the windward position and his faster ships he could stop and start the engagement at will and he had two good reasons for holding off. One was his knowledge that Spanish superiority would be overwhelming if the two fleets got to grappling at close quarters in the old style of naval warfare. The other was to conserve his powder. He had faith in his new style ships and his new style armament, but this first encounter had shown him that the tight Spanish crescent formation with the strong ships protecting the weaker would not be easily broken and at best they had many days fighting in front of them. The English were relying on long-range gunnery. They boasted a rate of fire three times that of the Spanish gunners. Yet they were even more short of ammunition than they were of food. Drake had reckoned that they sailed with ball and powder enough for one and a half days' fighting and it has been calculated that there was more gunpowder aboard the ships of the invading force than there was available in the whole of England at that time. So Howard bided his time and, using his ships like so many sheep dogs, slowly shepherded the great Spanish flock before him until, to the watchers on the Plymouth shore, it disappeared to the east behind the outline of the Mewstone rock.

There was relief in Plymouth which had expected to be one of the prime targets for a landing, and perhaps the bells of the parish church of St Andrews at the top of the old town rang out in rejoicing. It is a building with many Armada associations, rebuilt after being gutted during the air raids of the Second World War, but happily with much of the old structure surviving. The Yorkshireman, Martin Frobisher, who was commanding the biggest English ship, the *Triumph* of 1,100 tons, and who died of wounds in another battle, was buried here, or part of him was while the rest was interred in London. Drake and Howard took Communion here before the battle. The most intriguing relic is that commonly referred to as the Drake Graffiti, on a window ledge by the south door. Drake arrived back in Plymouth from his profitable circumnavigation in November 1580 and was knighted by the Queen the following April on board the *Golden Hind* at Greenwich. At the same time he was granted a coat of arms symbolic of his deed, a ship surmounting a globe from which is drawn a cord encircling the world. This graffiti, which is thought may have been done with the point of a plasterer's trowel, may be a crude representation of the coat of arms or may have been an attempt at a graphic explanation of the voyage, perhaps to untutored listeners. Nobody knows. It was uncovered during the restoration of the church and a sixteenth-century date has been vouchsafed by experts. Certainly Drake came to this church with his captains in thanksgiving after the defeat of the Armada and for several years afterwards on the anniversary of the sighting, July 19th. On these occasions he came in procession with the Corporation whom he, in another flamboyant gesture, had arranged should wear official red gowns. The Mayor and Corporation of Plymouth, complete with red gowns, continued to walk in procession to St Andrews on Armada Day for another two hundred years, but then the custom was sadly dropped.

This is a magnificent city church as befits a great city. Its historical associations are many, but even the most enthusiastic researcher is apt to forget them for a moment to gaze at the six windows by John Piper which became its crowning glory in the post-war restoration.

5

SEA DOGS OF DEVON

And tell old England to her face,
If she is great to fame,
'Twas good old heart of Devon oak
That made her glorious name.

(Edward Capern, the postman poet of Bideford, 1858)

We left the Armada disappearing from sight to the east of Plymouth and before rejoining it will make a diversion in search of a few more Armada reminders in Devon. One stop we unfortunately cannot make is at *HMS Drake*, one of the navy's 'stone frigates'. *HMS Drake*, like all Royal Navy shore establishments named and run like a ship, is the home base for personnel attached to Devonport to which they return between postings. Among her wardroom treasures is the sword of the illustrious sailor whose name she bears, the one with which Queen Elizabeth knighted him on board the *Golden Hind* at Greenwich. The royal arms are engraved on it, together with those of Drake, and alongside it stands an unusual drinking vessel fashioned from coconut shells, which must have been something of a curiosity when he brought them home. These precious relics are never on public view, even on special occasions like Navy Days, and the sword rarely leaves the guardianship of *HMS Drake*'s commanding officer. One of the rare occasions was when Queen Elizabeth the Second used it to knight Sir Francis Chichester at Greenwich on the completion of his single-handed circumnavigation in the yacht *Gypsy Moth*. Another may be for the fourth centenary Armada celebrations.

One call worth making before leaving the city is to the parish church of St Budeaux, hard by the approach road to the Tamar Bridge which carries the holiday traffic into Cornwall. It is the go-ahead parish church of a busy residential area, though the building itself stands in a quiet oasis of green. Here on July 4th 1569, Drake, at the age of thirty, married Mary Newman from across the river in Saltash. A copy of their marriage certificate is framed by the door. Poor Mary endured her husband's long absences and no doubt his violent eruptions of temper, but hopefully enjoyed her reward when he made her Lady Drake and purchased Buckland Abbey as a country residence befitting their improved status.

Buckland Abbey lies on the edge of Dartmoor, a mile or two west of the main Plymouth to Tavistock road where it passes through Yelverton. It houses another famous Armada relic, Drake's Drum. This happily is accessible to all, since the building now belongs to the National Trust. Originally it was a Cistercian abbey built in 1278. After the Dissolution it was acquired by the family of Sir Richard Grenville who sold it to Drake in 1581 for the sum of £3,000. Thereafter it remained in the hands of the Drake family for 350 years.

The drum can be found in the Great Hall in a large glass case, its appearance rather faded and looking as if it could do with a fresh coat of varnish, but perhaps the experts advise against it. It is a splendid drum nevertheless, a side drum of the sort used by infantry regiments in the sixteenth century, standing nearly 2ft (.6m) tall and 15in (38cm) in diameter. The vallum heads are supported on a barrel of walnut with ash bands, this being decorated with Drake's heraldic achievements. If the date ascribed to it is correct it could not, as the tale has it, have been aboard his flagship the *Revenge* during the Armada campaign, but it might well have accompanied his last fatal voyage when he was 'slung atween the round shot in Nombre Dios Bay'. Apart from fine clothes and the other trappings of affluence Drake loved music. On the *Golden Hind* voyage, started when his purse was not such a deep one, he had shipped musicians, which was quite a luxury, though you can bet they were also useful hands on deck. So it would have been in his nature to order a magnificent drum and perhaps it was even used to 'beat to quarters' when a scrap was imminent.

But almost certainly Drake didn't in his dying moments give the order:

> Take my drum to England
> Hang it by the shore
> Strike it when your powder's running low,

because what was preoccupying him when the dysentery had mortally weakened that rugged form was the clarification of his will, to make sure that his estates (and by this time he had properties in London and all over Plymouth as well as Buckland) passed securely to his younger brother Thomas, a faithful companion and lieutenant through most of his adventures. Drake's poor first wife Mary had lived to enjoy being lady of the manor at Buckland for only two years and he had married again a couple of years later, a more aristocratic lady this time, Elizabeth Sydenham the good-looking daughter of Sir George Sydenham of Somerset. The Sydenhams seem to have regarded Drake as a bit beneath them socially, but were not at all averse to getting their hands on his money, so Drake in his last hours signed a deed ensuring that most of his property went to his brother. As Drake had no children by either marriage it was through Thomas's descendants that the name survived at Buckland. That deed can also be found in the Great Hall and together with it the commission from the Queen authorising the famous raid on Cadiz, complete with its royal seal nearly six inches in diameter, both of these relics more valuable to historians than the more romantic drum.

The legend of the drum has even more tenuous origins than the game of bowls. It has two forms. One is that the drum can be heard to roll in warning when England is in danger, though the glass case must rather mute the call to arms. The other is that if struck in the hour of national danger, the spirit of Drake

Lizard Point, Cornwall — the Armada's first sight of England

Landewednack, most southerly parish church in Britain. When the Armada came its sermons were still being preached in Cornish

On Manhay Beacon, near Helston — the granite hut that sheltered the beacon lookouts

Looking across Fowey river to Gribbin Head — in the distance Dodman Point beneath which the Armada anchored

Rame Head with the chapel whose hermit was paid to tend the warning beacon

The remains of Plymouth's Castle Quadrate

St Andrew's Church, Plymouth, rich in Armada associations

Second-best Drake statue: Plymouth had to make do with this copy of Tavistock's to stand on the Hoe

New Street, Plymouth, little changed since it was packed with seamen on their way to join the ships that beat the Armada

The restored Merchants House, Plymouth, now a museum

Restored Elizabethan garden in New Street, Plymouth; Drake's house nearby would have had one very similar

St Budeaux Church on the outskirts of Plymouth where Drake was married

Buckland Abbey; it houses Drake's Drum, waiting to be struck in England's hour of need

Hope Cove and the rocks under Bolt Tail where the Spanish ship which came back by mistake ended its days

Hope Cove village, looking much as it did when the survivors of the
Spanish hospital ship came ashore

Start Point, Devon, off which the English fleet might have lost the battle
because of the light that failed

Dartmouth Castle; enlarged in time for the Armada, its guns were still defending the river in 1939–45

Giving an idea of life aboard an Armada ship, a replica of the *Golden Hind* in Brixham harbour

The Black Hole of Torquay? The Spanish Barn where four hundred Spanish prisoners were housed

Topsham, near Exeter, beside whose now silent quays three English ships were fitted out for the Armada

Portland Castle whose walls hid stolen property from one of the Spanish ships

Portland Bill; it provided the best grandstand view of the fighting along the south coast

Remains of the base of Lowestoft's beacon, a typical East Anglian amalgam of mortar and flint, now supporting the shaft of an old anchor (*copyright David Butcher*)

The militia armour that waits for the call to come again in the parish church of Mendlesham, Suffolk (*copyright Diss Express*)

Battle Honours board of the aircraft carrier HMS *Ark Royal* (*photo by Petty Officer Ken Rixon, Crown copyright reserved*)

The superb Armada Jewel given by Elizabeth to her Treasurer of War and one of her few tokens of recognition (*copyright Victoria and Albert Museum*)

Queen Elizabeth depicted on one of the Armada medals. She didn't give many away to the men who did the fighting (*reproduced by courtesy of the Trustees of the British Museum*)

Jug in Weymouth Museum; it may have held wine that slaked the thirst of Spanish sailors (*copyright Weymouth Museum*)

Weymouth's chest; did it once hold the gold of the stricken San Salvador? (*copyright Weymouth Museum*)

The Captain of the London Militia in his tent at Tilbury, depicted on his memorial in St Helen's Church, Bishopsgate, London

will return from that celestial haven where all good sailors rest and put the enemy to flight, as he did the Spaniards. There is no firm evidence that the story existed in any written form before it appeared from the pen of the Victorian barrister and poet Sir Henry Newbolt who found much of his inspiration in heroic deeds on land and sea. Where he got the idea is not known, but the poem first appeared in a collection called *Admirals All* in 1897 at a time when patriotic fervour was being kindled by rumblings of war with France. Devonians are fond of spinning a good yarn and many a pot of scrumpy might have been earned relating this one to credulous London gentry long before Newbolt heard it and turned it into a popular recitation piece (to the misery of thousands of schoolchildren in the days when learning poems by heart was an essential ingredient of Eng. Lit. education). It improved in the view of many after Sir William Walton set it to music.

Even more difficult to trace than the origins of the drum's legend is any suggestion that its mystical properties have ever been put to the test. There have after all been several occasions when it might have been useful. It would be satisfying to record, for instance, that in 1940 Winston Churchill despatched a secret escort from Downing Street to Devon: 'Sh . . . sh . . . shend for the drum [one can almost hear that characteristic slurred growl] for our powder is sh . . . sh . . . shurely running low'. Alas, the thought does not seem to have occurred even to that grand master of the dramatic gesture. Unless of course Drake's Drum was a secret weapon so highly classified that even under the Thirty Year Rule its use cannot be divulged.

If the drum is of doubtful efficacy there is no doubt about the usefulness or the authenticity of the next memento of the great mariner to be found on this exploration. Even if the Armada had never happened and the rest of the world had never heard of Francis Drake, he would still be remembered by the people of Plymouth as the man who gave the city its first water supply by tapping the River Meavy near his Buckland estates and channelling it through an artificial watercourse into the town. It is still there and Drake's Leat as it is known can be followed for much of its course.

In the year he occupied Buckland, Drake was made Mayor of Plymouth and it was then that he first proposed the idea. Fresh water was a constant problem to expanding communities, especially when large fleets of ships had to be supplied. An Act of Parliament was obtained granting the corporation permission to proceed, but with the preoccupations of the Spanish threat it was not until 1590 that Drake cut the first sod and a gang of Dartmoor tin miners set to work cutting the 18½ mile (30km) long channel which was finished four or five months later. Drake received a fee of £300 for organising the whole enterprise, but out of that he had to pay for labour, materials and compensation to owners of land the leat crossed. Critics have said that it was just another of his moneymaking schemes, but Plymouth had reason to be satisfied with the bargain because Drake's Leat remained the main source of water for an ever growing population for over three hundred years, until superceded by the modern Burrator Reservoir in 1898. A pleasant walk of half a dozen miles (9.6km) can be had following the leat from Burrator Gorge below the present reservoir dam wall and it appears at various places on the open moorland north of the city. The extant stretches have been located and described by the late Eric Hemery in his book *Walking the Dartmoor Waterways*.

Like so much else to do with Drake and the Armada the leat has its legend. Drake is supposed to have ridden to the spot where it was to start then turning his horse towards Plymouth spurred it into a gallop, whereupon the water followed him into the city. The practical reality of the enterprise and effort of cutting through that granite encrusted landscape is remembered every year by the people of Plymouth at an event known as the Fyshinge Feast. The Lord Mayor, accompanied by the Chairman of South West Water Authority, the modern custodians of the leat, gather by its banks with councillors and invited guests and drink a toast in an ancient silver goblet filled from the pure waters of the stream, 'To the pious memory of Sir Francis Drake'. Then with goblets charged with something a little stronger they drink another toast, 'May the descendants of him who brought us water, never want wine.'

Half a dozen miles (9.6km) northwards brings us to Tavistock where the Boehm statue (which Plymouth had to make do with a second best copy of) guards the junction of the Plymouth road. The place where Francis Drake was born is less conspicuously tucked away a mile and a half (2.5km) down the road. There is no restored 'birthplace' to visit such as Stratford-on-Avon offers tourists, but in the lush corner of the valley of the River Tavy where Crowndale Farm stands it needs little imagination to furnish the spot where El Draque first saw the light of day. The present farmhouse is nineteenth century, but it bears a small blue plaque recording Drake's birth at this spot. Members of the Drake family had been there since the reign of Henry the Seventh as tenants of Lord Russell, progenitor of the Dukes of Bedford of Woburn Abbey. This is not a fact that unduly impresses the present occupier of Crowndale, Mrs Emse Toop, for her own family on both sides have farmed the land hereabouts as Bedford tenants for about the same length of time. She was born there in 1915 and as a little girl remembers the fuss when gentry and gold-braided admirals came to unveil the plaque which her father had agreed to have on the wall. She kindly produces photographs of the event for the little trickle of pilgrims who turn up every year.

There is a good deal of doubt about whether Drake was born in the farmhouse or in a cottage on the farm. Mrs Toop says her outbuildings bear evidence of an older dwelling that might have been the one burned down by the sectarian mob. At any rate it was somewhere near this spot that Francis was born, first of the twelve children of pious Edmund. Lord Russell stood godfather and may have been a distant family connection, but the Drakes had never been more than yeoman stock and Edmund, who had been to sea, was only a latecomer to

Crowndale which his brother farmed.

From Tavistock the A386 skirts the north-west flank of Dart-moor to Okehampton whose Town Hall has another of those numerous pieces of furniture which go by the name of Armada chests and which was being confidently claimed as a genuine relic in the last century. The Clerk to the Council, Mr D. C. Voaden, said there is no record of it in the council's archives and he has never met an inhabitant who claimed to know its story. On the other hand it has never been examined by any expert and discredited, so it continues to stand four square in front of the marble fireplace in the council chamber while Okehampton debates the blessings soon to come from its long awaited bypass.

It is worth continuing the northward journey however if only to remind ourselves that Devon has two coasts and it was not only the one that faces the Channel that found the ships and men to meet the Spaniards. The thriving port of the north was Bideford, as it indeed still is, and by April 1588 it had already had six ships requisitioned. The government kept a register of all ships over 100 tons which might be used in emergency as well as details of 150 shipowners and 2,000 seamen in Devon. It didn't take the invention of the computer to put bureaucracy in the information business! At the time, three of Bideford's best ships were already victualled ready for an American adven-ture and the local merchants loudly protested about the losses they would suffer from this interference with trade. Neverthe-less three sailed for Plymouth, while three others were retained to keep watch on the Bristol Channel where they had a private brush with a lone Spanish raider in June.

Those that sailed for Plymouth included the *Tiger* and the *Virgin God Save Her*, both 200 tons and belonging to Sir Richard Grenville who also supplied the *John* from the neigh-bouring port of Barnstaple. In fact, Barnstaple claims that most of the ships came from there. They have put up a plaque in Queen Anne's Walk to give the details, and stake their claim to the glory claimed by Bideford. Sir Richard Grenville does not seem to have played an active role in the Armada, at least at sea. His immortality was to come later at 'Flores in the Azores' when he died pitting the *Revenge* against the entire Spanish fleet, inspiring Tennyson's ballad 'The Revenge', which is almost as well known as 'Drake's Drum' and certainly better poetry. His son John led the little fleet which sailed from Bideford and on this occasion it was Drake's flag which flew in the *Revenge*, which was one of the Queen's regular navy ships, 500 tons and carrying 250 personnel. Downstream, at the mouth of the estuary in the picturesque port of Appledore from where some of the last of the British trading schooners sailed, they did their bit too. What they did has not survived in the records, but the Queen granted Appledore status as a free port as a reward, one of the few marks of favour she did bestow to mark her victory. Appledore's North Devon Maritime Museum also has one of those ubiquitous chests and a pair of cannon too, but cautiously says they are 'of the Armada period'.

We left the Armada on the evening of that summer Sunday shaping a course to take it past the next headland, Start Point, another fine vantage point with exhilarating walks. Before picking up the trail there it is worth paying another visit to investigate the unfortunate story of the only ship in the Armada to sail up Channel twice.

Hope Cove lies under the shadow of Bolt Tail, a dark and glowering cliff face on the east side of Bigbury Bay, 15 miles (24km) beyond Plymouth by sea. In a car you can find it by leaving the A379 at Kingsbridge, but walkers have the best approach following the heady clifftop path which ascends the loftier eminence of Bolt Head from Salcombe, then dropping into Hope Cove over the Tail. Despite the scattering of modern bungalows around the hillside, Hope on a quiet day can look like the tiny natural fishing haven it has been for the last four hundred years and more, but it was far from quiet on the night of October 28th 1588 when the 500 ton bulk of the *San Pedro Mayor* crashed her weary timbers into the rocks there.

The *San Pedro* was one of the hospital ships of the Spanish fleet. She set off from Spain with a crew of 30 sailors, carrying 100 soldiers and 50 sick bay staff. When the Armada scattered before the gales after the final engagement off Gravelines she survived the northabout journey round Scotland and Ireland that proved fatal for so many of her companions, but then either as a result of damage, adverse winds or faulty navigation she sailed back up Channel instead of heading for the Spanish coast and tore out her bottom on the rocks under Bolt Tail. Most of the men aboard managed to get ashore and the better-class ones were lodged at Kingsbridge to await ransom.

The *San Pedro*'s role in the fleet did not make her one of the fabulous treasure ships of Armada legend, but that did not prevent official anxiety about 'the great pilfering and spoils that the country people made', as the Deputy Lieutenant Sir George Cary reported to London. Money and plate was taken from the survivors' chests and clothing as they came ashore. As the ship was full of water to the upper decks as she lay on the rocks her cargo of 'drugs and other pothecary stuff' worth 6,000 ducats was soon spoilt, according to the report, but two constables were set searching ashore for 'certain bezoar stones and other simples' (apparently much prized remedies) which had gone missing. Hope Cove has seen a great many wrecks since, but perhaps none so profitable as the luckless hospital ship that came round twice.

The walker who returns over Bolt Tail and Head to Salcombe can cross by ferry to Portlemouth where the coast path resumes round Prawle Point and thence to Start. By road the journey necessitates a return to Kingsbridge and then to Torcross from where a narrow lane is signposted to Start Point. Cars can be parked in a field at the end of the track, leaving a gentle down-hill stroll of half a mile (.8km) to the lighthouse perched on the end of the razor's edge extremity of the point. It was not there of course when the Armada sailed by in slow procession through the long evening, and by the time the English pursuers were in view 2 miles (3km) astern it was growing dark, but in these battle conditions none of the ships showed lights. There was one light to guide the fleet however and that became one of the most controversial topics of the whole campaign for the simple reason that it wasn't there. To follow the story of 'the light that failed' we must recall the events of earlier in the day.

It will be remembered that the first casualty of the battle, as the result of an internal explosion, was the *San Salvador*. Confusion naturally ensued in the Spanish ranks as other ships turned to her aid and the English Lord Admiral took this opportunity to press his attack closer, using his command of the windward position. So far the English gunnery was accurate, but at the range they had to keep, to avoid the close-quarters encounter which might be their undoing, it was not inflicting very much damage. Now as the English moved in closer the brunt of the accurate gunnery was borne by the 768 ton *Santa Ana*, flagship of Juan Martinez de Recalde, an experienced and brilliant seaman who was ashamed of his chief's defensive tactics when he should be doing his damnedest to close and grapple with the enemy. As it was he obeyed his orders to cover the rear while the crippled *San Salvador* was huddled in tow into the protective cover of the fleet. After two hours of bombardment Recalde's ship was damaged enough to need aid herself. A brother Knight of Santiago, Don Pedro de Valdes, turned his great 1,000 ton *Nuestra Señora del Rosario* to go to her assistance, but in doing so collided in that great mêlée of ships with one of his own squadron, losing his bowsprit and foremast and becoming unmanageable. There were now four Spanish ships crippled, only one due to enemy action. As best they could they limped along with the rest as the sun sank behind the Cornish hills.

Off Start Point, Lord Howard of Effingham decided to keep up his cautious pursuit, making sure that Sidonia's timidity was not a blind for a surprise assault further along the coast. He established the sailing order for the night and ordered Drake to lead the English ships showing, at the stern of the *Revenge*, just one lantern which the others could follow. A keen eyed watcher on Start Point might have seen that solitary pinpoint, but not for long. To the confusion and consternation of the watch-keepers in the other ships the light they were following suddenly disappeared and the *Revenge* was lost sight of. Some captains kept on course as best they could while others hove-to or reduced sail until they knew what was happening, which did not become clear until late next day. In Dartmouth, the next stop on our coastwise journey, reached along the straight road between Slapton Ley and the sea, the consequences were still reverberating over a month later.

From that lovely port, now so bright on a summer day with the sails of countless yachts, could be seen early in September 1588 eight boatloads of Brixham fishermen straining at their oars as they towed into the river the huge hulk of the *Nuestra Señora del Rosario*, the flagship of the Andalusian squadron which was so badly damaged in collision while turning to the assistance of Recalde. She was the first and richest prize of the Armada battle and it was for her that Francis Drake had surreptitiously doused the great stern lantern on the *Revenge* and disappeared into the night. Not until Monday afternoon, when they were halfway across Lyme Bay, had he rejoined his colleagues, excusing his absence with a story of strange sails seen in the night which he thought must be investigated in case they were the enemy doubling back, but which turned out to be innocent German merchantmen. Then, fortuitously, he had come across the *Rosario* left straggling behind and Pedro de Valdes had surrendered to him. Few seem to have doubted that he had deliberately slipped off in search of this juicy prize so ripe for plucking. Martin Frobisher in the *Triumph* was beside himself with rage. He called Drake a traitor and a coward and threatened to make him 'spend the best blood in his belly'. Lord Admiral Howard forbearingly made no issue of his apparent desertion of a trusted post, but some writers say they can detect cooler references to Drake in subsequent despatches.

While Drake had entertained de Valdes aboard the *Revenge* in gentlemanly fashion as chivalry demanded and discussed over the wine how much he might be ransomed for, the *Rosario* with her 422 sailors and soldiers aboard had been taken into Tor Bay under a prize crew and kept at anchor there by adverse weather until September 7th when the Brixham fishermen were persuaded to tow her into the River Dart for a fee of 26s. Here the Deputy Lieutenant, Sir George Cary, who had been having the devil of a job to stop her being pilfered, was able to mount a proper guard and take a full inventory for prize money purposes. Later the *Rosario* was patched up and sailed round to Chatham, but she was broken up when found too ungainly for use in the English fleet.

Her arrival was not the first excitement of the Armada for Dartmouth which had been an important port since the Middle Ages, its defence as vital as that of Plymouth. In its time the castle guarding the harbour mouth represented the country's most advanced technology, being the first specially designed for artillery. But that was in 1481 at the dawn of the gunpowder age and during the years of mounting tension with Spain the rock floors of the basements were dug down and back into the hillside to make more room for manipulating the improved sixteenth-century guns. The castle is still there, a mile (1.6km) or so along roads which twist up and down the creeks out of the town towards the mouth of the estuary. It clings to the cliff, cheek by jowl with the old church of St Petroc and if you look across the river from its battlements you can see its twin defender Kingswear Castle. Between them they would have caught intruding ships in a murderous cross-fire. With still further improvements in firing power Kingswear Castle became redundant later in the century when it was reckoned that the guns of Dartmouth could cover the approaches on their own. Kingswear Castle is a private residence now, while Dartmouth Castle is an English Heritage building open to the public and displaying an interesting exhibition of its historic defensive role, which lasted until the Second World War when 4.7in guns were mounted and men in khaki kipped down in the Elizabethan gunners' quarters.

The gunners of 1940 did not have to worry about old Jawbones, the name their predecessors gave to the chain which had to be hauled across the river mouth to halt any hostile vessel that slipped through the gunfire and which, as we saw in an earlier chapter, had been appropriated many years ago from the Cornishmen in Fowey. It was stretched between Dartmouth Castle and another old fort, Gomerock, on the Kingswear side whose remaining stones are marked still by the grooves through which the chain ran; this too is on private property. As a further precaution another castle had also been erected in Dartmouth itself at Bayard's Cove where the lower car ferry from Kingswear lands. Its ruins, free to casual clambering inspection, bound a quayside area so perfectly preserved that it has become a desirable location for makers of period films. It was probably alongside here that the 60 ton *Hart* with 70 men under James Houghton and the 140 ton *Crescent* with 75 men were fitted out and victualled for the great adventure. These were the ships which Dartmouth, together with Totnes up the river, were charged by the government to provide, but there were also volunteers sent by local owners like Sir John Gilbert, the site of whose family seat up river at Greenway became better known as the home of Agatha Christie. They included the *Samaritan*, 250 tons, the *Unicorn*, 76 tons, and the *Elizabeth*, 40 tons, carrying 170 men between them. Nowhere in England apart from Plymouth and the Thames bustled so much with Armada activity as Dartmouth. Twenty pages of the town's accounts recording what it all cost are still preserved in the County Record Office.

Foe and friend slipped past Dartmouth in the night and would have been seen by a watcher at dawn on Monday morning filling the seascape from Berry Head which the motorist can reach by crossing by one of the two ferries over the Dart. For walkers the lower ferry is best for access to the next stretch of the coast path.

It is said that the 190ft (58m) high top of Berry Head commands a view on a clear day of 800sq miles (2,072km²) of sea, and how the 425 men on *Ark Royal* must have wished for such a view that Monday morning, because as the dawn light flooded Tor Bay they realised they were surrounded by enemy ships. Some half a dozen English ships were huddled round the Lord High Admiral, but of Drake in the *Revenge* and of all the other ships who had slowed down or lost direction when they could no longer see the lantern, there was no sign. By good fortune or good seamanship and the disinclination of the Spanish commander to engage, they extricated themselves, but it was some time before Howard could organise his squadrons for an orderly pursuit of the Spanish formations now headed for Portland Bill, 42 miles (68km) away.

As we have seen it was late afternoon before Drake caught up from his profitable diversion, and with a strengthening wind the fleets were then lost to view from Berry Head. The headland has no visible Armada monuments today, but it has plenty of history of other periods to interest the visitor, apart from the attraction of its windswept grassy walks. It has in fact a whole series of forts built at various times in the eighteenth and nineteenth centuries, the chief of them with ramparts and batteries well preserved. Another curiosity of Berry Head is its lighthouse which is the highest, the smallest and the deepest in England, a hat trick of records which could create too long a diversion to explain here.

Below Berry Head lies Brixham, mother of the trawling industry and thriving on fishing still. Its main place in the history books was gained exactly a century after the Armada when William of Orange landed there in a more successful 'invasion' we call the Glorious Revolution. It is worth a stop on the Armada trail however because it is one of the few places where we can gain an idea what life was like afloat for the 30,000 Spaniards and 16,000 Englishmen whose progress we have been following, because in Brixham harbour is moored and open to the public as a tourist attraction a replica of the *Golden Hind*, the ship in which Drake sailed round the world. Although it was made for filming a television series in 1954 and therefore with features above the waterline faked in plywood, the subsequent owners have spent the visitors' fees carefully rebuilding her in relatively authentic fashion. The original *Golden Hind* was not in the Armada fleet and some of the leading ships on both sides were six or eight times her size, but of the 197 English ships officially listed as taking part around one hundred were of this size or considerably less. It is salutary to stand below decks with barely headroom and reflect that seventy men existed in such cramped space, reduced even further with barrels of powder and stores, overrun with rats and stinking with filth. Here more than anywhere can be found the reality of the Armada for the common mariner.

Half a dozen miles (9.6km) along the coast a dual carriageway flanks the broad sweep of Tor Bay and on the left, just before reaching Torquay, stands a building amid the municipal greensward that saw more of the Spanish invaders than anywhere else in England. It is known, as it has been since 1588, as Spanish Barn. Poor old conscientious George Cary commandeered it to house the four hundred prisoners from the *Rosario* and it might almost have gone down in history as the Black Hole of Torquay but for the fact that the prisoners were used to even more crowded conditions, as we discovered on the replica *Golden Hind*.

Torquay at this time was no more than a few fishermen's hovels, but Torre Abbey had stood nearby since the twelfth century and it was its great tithe barn that Cary used, sending the current owner who had bought the place after the Dissolution one of the eighty-five pipes of wine from the Spaniard's hold as compensation for the trouble. The rest seemed to be disappearing before he could get them ashore under lock and key, but they were the least of his worries for it had emerged from questioning the prisoners that the *Rosario* was one of the four most richly laden Spanish ships, carrying 'a chest of the king's wherin there was 52,000 ducats, of which chest Don Pedro de Valdes had one key and the King's Treasurer the other . . . and many other of the gentlemen had good store of money aboard'.

From his home at Cockington (now swallowed up in Torquay)

Cary wrote urgently to London for orders about the disposal of his unwanted guests. 'Their provision which is left to sustain them is very little and nought' he told Walsingham. 'Their fish savours so it is not to be eaten and their bread full of worms. The people's charity to them, coming with so wicked an intent, is very cold; so that if there be not order taken by your Lordships they must starve.' If legend is to believed not all of the people's charity was as cold as he reported, for it used to be said that some rather darker complexions than are common to Devon were seen among subsequent generations of local inhabitants.

At any rate they were an embarrassment one way or another, many being weak and several finding their last resting place beneath the green lawns and flower beds that now slope down to the road. Lacking any instructions from London and tired of feeding them at his own expense, Cary summoned a company of militia to march half of them to the bridewell at Exeter and the rest he put back aboard the ship to manage 'upon such victuals as do remain in the said ship'.

An attempted escape from the Exeter party left Devon with another Armada inheritance, though only those with strong psychic powers should bother to look for it. In St Marychurch, which occupies the hilltop between Torquay and Babbacombe, some of the soldiers made a break for it and one was killed in the struggle. His broken-hearted wife was reported to haunt Westhill Road in search of him, dressed of course, being Spanish, in a mantilla. The last recorded sighting of the poor widow was in 1932 when the Devonshire Association published a report by one of its members of a first hand account from one of the residents. 'I zeed her Mum' said the woman 'with my own eyes and her shruck [shrieked] something orful and I was all of a tremble, tooth and nail'. Were it not for the scholarly reputation of the Devonshire Association one could be forgiven for thinking that it all sounded a little too much like stage Mummerset to be genuine, but it was half a century ago. Westhill Road didn't seem much like a place for wandering spirits when I went in search of the lady in the mantilla. The houses that stand there now aren't occupied by the kind of people who say 'mum', nor yet 'sir', to any passing investigator and they don't speak the rich dialect of Uncle Tom Cobley. Alas I could find no-one who had heard of, let alone seen, the one and only ghost of the Spanish Armada. I hoped that perhaps since 1932 she had found the spirit of her gallant husband and they were both repatriated to rest in peace.

6

SOUTH COAST ALERT

And the men that helped them do it, helped them still to hold the sea,
Men from Itchenor and Shoreham, men from Deal and Winchelsea,
Looked out happily from Heaven and cheered to see the work
Of their grandson's grandson's grandsons on the beaches of Dunkirk.

('The Other Little Boats' by Edward Shanks)

The deep indentation of Lyme Bay meant that little of the two
fleets could be seen by a watcher from the Devon shore, but a
traveller heading eastward towards Dorset to catch them up,
with the smoke still rising from the hilltops and the lanes noisy
with pot-valiant local musters, might have witnessed interesting sidelights on the country's reaction to its danger. Teignmouth for instance, the next port on from Torquay, was refusing
to pay. So was its neighbour Dawlish. They were far from being
alone. All over the country there were arguments about who
was going to meet the cost of fitting out the ships ordered by
central government.

Exeter had been instructed to find three ships to join Drake
in Plymouth and had requisitioned some which were about to
sail for a profitable voyage to Newfoundland, but didn't see why
only the city should lose by it. As a port authority, though not
as a local government unit, Exeter took in Teignmouth, Dawlish
and many other places as well including Kenton, a little village
near Dawlish; Exmouth and Lympstone on the Exe estuary; the
east Devon resorts of Sidmouth and Seaton, and the nearby
village of Colyton; plus Tiverton and Cullompton well to the
north of the city. Visiting some of these today, it is amazing to
think that they ever had sufficient water-borne trade to be

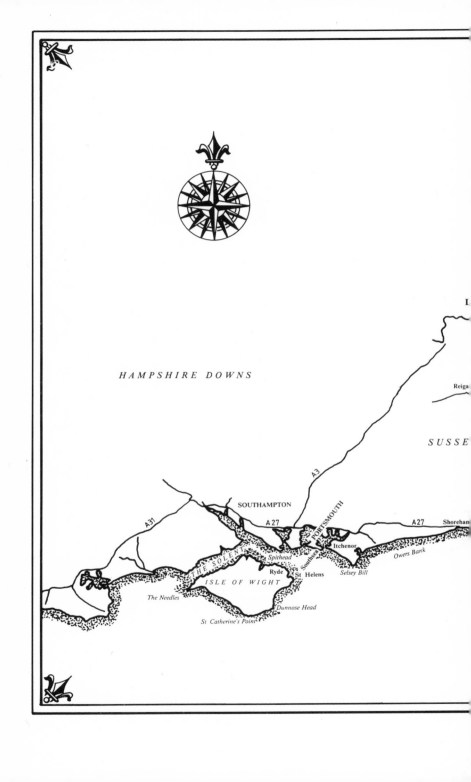

HAMPSHIRE DOWNS

SOUTHAMPTON

A 27

A 31

PORTSMOUTH

A 3

Spithead

THE SOLENT

Southsea

Itchenor

Ryde

St Helens

ISLE OF WIGHT

The Needles

Dunnose Head

St Catherine's Point

Selsey Bill

Owers Bank

A 27

Shoreham

SUSSE

Reiga

I

regarded even as out-ports, but they evidently did and Exeter was determined they should pay their share as they were 'places and creeks belonging to the port of Exeter whereunto the most number and best ships of the whole harbour doth belong' — in other words they could afford it. Every one of them refused to cough up on the grounds that the government order didn't include them by name, but only referred to Exeter. So in their fine Guildhall which still stands in High Street flanked by the modern mammoth shopping centre, the aldermen of Exeter led by the Mayor, Joseph Peryam, wrote to the Privy Council with many expressions of loyalty and humble duty pleading for clear orders to these awkward neighbours to make their contribution. Who paid up in the end is not clear, but some of them continued to chafe at Exeter jurisdiction over their waters for many years. When Teignmouth was made an independent port in 1853 they declared a public holiday and held a carnival in the streets.

The case of Topsham was rather different. This out-port was named in the original writ from London, but it still refused Exeter's demand for a contribution, which was not surprising because it had been in a state of feud with the city since time immemorial. Topsham stands lower down the Exe and was insignificant enough until 1282, when the Mayor of Exeter refused to pay a customary tithe of fish to the Countess of Devon who had her revenge by building a weir across the Exe, downstream of the city, known to this day as Countess Weir. This impediment to navigation caused great hardship in Exeter, but brought prosperity to Topsham which took over the handling of the wool export and wine import trades. Exeter merchants had to pay 5s a ton to get their goods by carrier's cart to and from Topsham and it was only twenty years before the Armada when, after nearly three hundred years, they won their trade back with the opening of England's first ship canal, the Exeter Canal which bypassed Countess Weir and opened up traffic again from the Exe into the city. Topsham's prosperity declined as a result so its townsfolk had an understandable aversion to helping Exeter foot the bill.

Happy to relate Topsham, or Apsam as it was called then, eventually recovered and prospered again until nearly the end of the Victorian age. The well-preserved houses of the ship-masters and builders with their trim gardens flanking the river belong to many periods, but here and there in quiet, narrow streets once busy with ropewalks, nail factories and sail lofts can be spotted a beam or doorway that might well have been in use when the *Bartholomew*, 130 tons, the *Rose*, 110 tons, and the little *Gift* of 25 tons, every one a Topsham ship, were fitted out alongside these quays and sent with 140 men as Exeter's con-tentious contribution to the defence of the realm.

Along the coast the Mayor of Lyme Regis, which had fitted out the *Jacob*, 90 tons and the *Revenge*, 60 tons (not Drake's flagship) and found 80 men to man them, was having similar difficulties winkling a share out of Axminster and Chard. Mayors all over England were in the same quandary. All through the summer their letters reached London complaining that the next town would not pay its share, or the charges would ruin them, or their contribution was more highly assessed than their neighbour's. Somehow the ships got to sea and the writers of endless local guide books testify to the patriotism of their ancestors in sending them, but the bundles of letters rest-ing in the State papers often tell a less wholehearted story.

Valuable time was wasted in the English fleet that Monday in reforming after the previous night's fiasco and it was late in the day before they had closed with the enemy rear at extreme range, by which time the entire cavalcade was clustered round Portland Bill. The shattered *San Salvador* had been abandoned after being stripped of all valuables and her crew taken off, all except some forty horribly burned wretches, whose condition turned the stomach of even that old campaigner and slave trader John Hawkins when he went aboard to take possession. He returned to the *Victory* and left the job in the hands of Flemying of the *Golden Hind*.

The Spanish commander also had reorganised his fleet and,

having decided that the ships following him must be pretty well all the English could muster, had put his own main strength in the rearguard. Still many of his captains were urging him to turn and destroy the English ships and counselled that at least they should have plans to take the Isle of Wight, which would make a secure base for their military operations. And still Medina Sidonia stood by the letter of his orders as he saw them. He would progress up Channel until he could make contact with the Duke of Parma in the Low Countries. To this end he ordered his ships to keep strictly on station in a new tighter formation and to emphasis the point he placed a master-at-arms equipped with a halter on every ship, with orders to hang the captain if the ship left its position in the formation for any reason whatever. Much later on this trail we shall find one wretched skipper who failed to obey.

From a distance the Isle of Portland looks like some giant dead cormorant sticking its scrawny neck out into the English Channel. After travelling through the lush rounded contours of Dorset it seems a gaunt place, torn apart for the famous stone which for centuries has been used for Britain's greatest buildings. London may boast St Paul's, but Portland has the hole in the ground it came out of. When the Armada came, Portland was still an island in all but the most pedantic definition, an 18 mile (29km) tramp along the foot-punishing shingle of the Chesil Bank from Abbotsbury being the only way to reach it by land. Normal traffic was by a short but perilous ferry-crossing where the saltwater lake, the Fleet, empties into Weymouth Bay. In the local museum at Church Ope Cove, housed in an attractive group of stone cottages, is the petition the Portlanders sent to the king two centuries later begging for a road bridge to connect them to the mainland. Because transport was such a problem all the stone was dug in earlier times out of the cliff edges and loaded straight into barges, so the quarrymen of Thomas Hardy's 'Isle of Slingers' probably had the best view of some of the tensest hours of the Armada drama, especially from Portland Bill at the island's southern tip.

It had been a still moonlit night and with first light on Tuesday there was no wind. This was a golden Spanish opportunity for they had a squadron of 4 great galleasses, each mounting 50 guns and propelled by 300 rowers. They were the classic ship with which Spain had won her greatest victories and in these conditions they could outmanoeuvre the becalmed English ships and pick them off one by one. Don Hugo de Moncada who commanded the galleasses pleaded with Sidonia to let him attack, but was refused and returned to his ship deeply offended. Then a deputation of other officers persuaded the duke that this really was the big chance and he changed his mind, but Moncada was in a huff and simply ignored the messages sent to him. Before he could be cajoled the wind sprang up and the opportunity was gone, but the Spanish captains could hardly believe their luck, because the new wind was from the north-east giving them the weather gauge. Not even Sidonia could hold back now and when his rearguard closed towards the enemy he followed in the *San Martin*.

What the watchers on Portland Bill saw then was the English van squadron, led by Frobisher in the *Triumph*, tacking inshore towards them in an effort to outflank the enemy and regain the windward position, a move in which they succeeded even though the ageing *Triumph* was the biggest and unhandiest of all the queen's ships. However, Howard's squadron attempting the same manoeuvre on a different tack did not make it and so Frobisher was cut off from his comrades, isolated dangerously close inshore. The great galleasses were at last unleashed and swooped on Frobisher's ships, but the hot-tempered Yorkshireman was nothing if not a fighter and a seaman. Cornered as he was with little sea room, he outsailed his attackers and halted their progress with his accurate gunnery. Meanwhile the main forces were exchanging their hottest fire so far. For the first time the two flagships were ranged against each other, the distance was closing to the advantage of the heavier Spanish armament and even boarding began to look a possibility. Perhaps more important Medina Sidonia had decided the time had come for confrontation, or that he could no longer avoid it. So throughout the morning of Tuesday, July 23rd, they fought under the lee of Portland Bill while the wind drifted them all slowly back to the westward. Thick smoke covered the water and the noise of the cannonades was a continuous roll of thunder. A Spanish account says that Howard poured five hundred shot into the *San Martin* and killed fifty men, but if this was typical of the rate of exchange it is remarkable that there were no ship losses on either side. Howard in fact was more preoccupied with keeping the range open while he worked to windward to reunite his divided forces and had every reason to conserve ball and powder as much as possible. Then around midday the smoke began to clear as the wind veered to the south and from the Bill could be seen fifty English sail bearing down upon the Spaniards, causing them once more to reform before a hail of fire and resume their easterly course, at the same time freeing Frobisher's ships from their bottleneck and relieving the pressure on Howard. It was Drake to the rescue, or so it seems.

Some of the less pro-Drake writers assert that there is no evidence that it was Drake, but by process of elimination it can hardly have been any other squadron ranging up towards the Bill. Professor Lewis argues cogently that Drake knew well the habit of the Channel winds which often begin to blow on shore in the forenoon and that he had positioned himself ready to swoop when the moment was ripe. In the *Relation of Proceedings* in the British Library, thought to be the nearest thing to an official report from Howard, it says only that 'a troop of her Majesty's ships and sundry merchants' assailed the Spanish fleet so sharply to the westward that they were all forced to give way and to bear room'. That neither Drake nor the *Revenge* are mentioned by name, when participants in several more trivial incidents are, has been attributed to that coolness which followed the lantern incident. There is little doubt that what could be seen from Portland Bill was a bit more of the old Drake magic being enacted, or more specifically his thrust and consummate seamanship.

Sitting on the end of Portland Bill today it is possible to see just what degree of seamanship was needed by both sides at that juncture, for they could not have chosen a more difficult place to have their first major engagement. The Portland Race is the fiercest and most extensive tide rip on the English south coast and at some states of the tide the sea boils like a cauldron as far as the eye can see, contorted waves running erratically in all directions. Powerful ships take little account of it today, but sailing vessels which did not give it a wide berth could be flung off course and tossed about like corks. The rocks of Portland loomed close, with the great shingle bank of the Chesil Beach on one side and the shallows of Weymouth Bay on the other. Tuesday's battleground straddled this uncomfortable stretch of sea and fighting continued sporadically between individual units until evening, when the whole circus had moved east-wards of the Bill. The Armada had lost its best chance, for even with the windward position and close fighting it had failed to grapple and board a single English ship. On the other hand it was itself relatively unscathed and still pursuing its eastward objective. So far as the English leaders and the defenders on shore knew, it might still attempt a landing anywhere.

But at any rate they could now stand easy in Portland Castle, another of Henry the Eighth's fortifications, which with later improvements overlooks the modern naval dockyard. The latter was a nineteenth-century innovation built in the days when the size of Queen Victoria's navy called for another Channel base between Plymouth and Portsmouth. Weymouth nestling in the corner of the bay was, in 1588, still waiting for George the Third to make it fashionable by patronage of its sea bathing. The mayor, Richard Pitt, was busy persuading London that it was 'much destitute' and couldn't afford to provide Her Majesty with 'two ships and one pinnace, men, munition and victuals for two months'. He assured the Privy Council they had been doing their bit, however, because 'of our own indus-try, to our very great charge, we have builded a platform for some defence of this town and country, at this instance not furnished with needful ordnance, by reason of our poverty'. Poor Weymouth never did get its cannon in time to point them at the passing Armada, but it did somehow find the ships, the *Galleon* of 100 tons and the *Katharine* of 66 tons. Three more Weymouth ships, all probably experienced privateers, sailed as volunteers — the *Heathen*, 60 tons, the *Golden Ryall*, 120 tons and the *Bark Sutton*, 70 tons — making altogether more than three hundred Weymouth men in the fray.

After the Armada had passed, Weymouth had another flurry of activity when Flemying of the *Golden Hind* anchored the *San Salvador* off shore. There wasn't much of value left aboard, but the mayor appropriated what little remained of her armament to supply the deficiency at the town battery. It amounted to 'eight pieces of brass, four old minions and two old fowlers' which the government eventually agreed the town could keep. The locals managed to grab one or two other useful things, despite an order from Lord Burghley to the local justices to see that everything was 'landed and safely preserved in some convenient storehouses'. The immediate concern however was to off-load her considerable remaining quantity of ball and powder and send it to answer the now desperate appeals from Howard for more ammunition.

It was a frantic job because the *San Salvador* was in such a state that ten men were employed day and night at the pumps to prevent her sinking in the bay and she was too deep draughted to bring into the river for unloading. Among those who managed to lay hands on some useful gear out of her was a man called Nicholas Jones, who was probably the commander of Portland Castle. He took possession of a new foresail and a dozen sweeps (huge oars) from the ship, with consequences that proved more serious than a loss of revenue to the Crown. When the danger from the Armada had passed it was decided to sail the *San Salvador* round to the royal dockyard at Portsmouth and the crew who were to take her went to Jones to get the gear back. Jones was unco-operative and it was not until they had been to the magistrates that he agreed to return it; but he went back on his word and when the crew, many of whom were local men, went to collect, Jones had disappeared from the castle and the *San Salvador*'s gear was nowhere to be found. So in mid November they had to sail the patched up *San Salvador* without a foresail and without sweeps, the latter the equivalent of an auxiliary engine to a modern sailing vessel. Much else was also missing because the local magistrates reported much stealing of ropes and casks and said that 'the disorder was very great'.

Among the missing items could have been a great chest now in Weymouth Museum which has always been said to be the treasure chest from the *San Salvador*. But although much else in his reports was vague, the Duke of Medina Sidonia did tell King Philip quite clearly that he had taken the great chest and all valuables from the hold of the *San Salvador* before she was abandoned, so there must be doubt about Weymouth's chest. However, it may have been easier in mid Channel for the Spanish seamen to transfer the gold from the *San Salvador* in smaller containers and leave this huge iron-bound piece of furniture behind, and with all the looting going on in Weymouth it might well have escaped the official inventory. Nobody can prove its authenticity, but neither has anyone yet disproved it. A humbler object in the museum is not disputed. It is one of the *San Salvador*'s wine jars.

The crew of fifty-seven men put into the leaking Spaniard took her along the Dorset coast and weathered St Aldhelm's Head, where perhaps the hermit in his tiny clifftop chapel, which is still there, said a prayer for them. They safely passed Anvil Point and the razor sharp Peveril Ledges off Swanage, where a Danish fleet met its end after Alfred the Great had beaten it in 877. Then somewhere off Studland the *San Salvador* gave up the struggle and went to the bottom, taking with her twenty-three men, six of them being wretched French and Fleming nationals who had been in the ship since she left Spain and endured all her miseries. Whether she was driven by a gale on to Old Harry Rocks, unable to claw off for lack of sweeps and a foresail, we do not know. Official correspondence of the time sadly lacks any such dramatic details. They were just taken for granted, part of men's everyday working lives. The thirty-four survivors however were in no doubt who was to blame. They had the luck to be picked up by a small man o'war which was at Studland and their opinion of the culpability of Mr Jones of Portland Castle was recorded by John Thomas, a dockyard official at Portsmouth with the title of Clerk of the Prick and Check: 'There be of his neighbours that are saved and others of the company, that will venture their lives whenever they meet him; for all those that are saved will depose that he was the casting away of the ship and the death of the men'.

From the round bump of Ballard Down above Studland the Armada and its pursuers could have been seen shaping a course towards the southern shore of the Isle of Wight. A mile or so over the sand dunes the present South West Coast Path, which has provided such a convenient route for following the Armada, comes to an end at Shell Bay at the mouth of Poole Harbour. In Poole the Mayor, John Bergman, like so many others had been pleading poverty due to 'the great decay and disability of this poor town by reason of embargoes, want of traffic, loss at sea and by pirates which have and continually do lie at Studland Bay'. In the end they offered the *Primrose*, 120 tons, and a small bark called the *Elephant*.

Along the coast in Hampshire, Southampton was penning much the same excuses and described itself as 'wonderfully decayed'. Its Solent neighbour Portsmouth however was already a long established naval base and is an important call on this Armada trail. Unlike Plymouth it doesn't have an Elizabethan atmosphere because most of its extant historical associations belong to the period two hundred years later when fighting sail had reached the peak of its development. The spirit of Drake presides over Plymouth, but the spirit of Nelson presides over Portsmouth — and thereby hangs a tale.

Drake, as we have seen, was a rumbustious, full-blooded chap, a good rugby scrum half if ever there was one. What is more 'Drake he was a Devon man', as everyone knew. Now down in Devon they could never really stomach the idea that the victor of Trafalgar, Copenhagen and the Nile, the Number One naval hero of all time, could really be such a pale, sickly, emaciated looking little bloke — and from Norfolk at that! There could only be one explanation. Nelson's frail body really hid the spirit of Francis Drake, come back in his country's hour of need 'as he promised long ago'. This fanciful yarn is told in a poem called 'The Admiral's Ghost' written in 1908 by Alfred Noyes, inspired no doubt by Newbolt's earlier work. So far as anyone knows its origins were entirely in the poet's imagination, but it is an amusing party piece that deserves to be better known.

Whatever the case, it is the Georgian navy that dominates Pompey's past as surely as the yards of Nelson's *Victory* tower over the dockyard, but that is changing. HMS *Victory* has recently gained two companions. One is HMS *Warrior* of 1860, the first steam-driven iron battleship which marked the end of the wooden walls, discovered rotting in Milford Haven and restored by the Maritime Trust. The other is the *Mary Rose*, the pride of Henry the Eighth's navy, which was lifted with amazing skill and dedication from beneath the mud of the Solent where she had rested for four hundred years. She, too, represented an important innovation in naval warfare, being the first ship with gunports cut in her sides, but when much was expected of her during a French attack she mysteriously sank before the King's own eyes. It happened forty-one years before the Armada, but from her the visitor to Portsmouth can learn a great deal about the ships which fended off Spain and about the men who sailed them. Lying undisturbed beneath the mud the *Mary Rose* became an incredible time capsule, preserving the weapons, clothes, tools, eating utensils, instruments and a vast store of other artefacts on board. Unlike our own age, the pace of change in the sixteenth century was very slow, so there would have been hardly any difference between the contents of the *Mary Rose* and those of the ships fitted out in 1588. All these objects have been skilfully restored and interpreted for display in the Mary Rose Museum and the hull will be very slowly and carefully rebuilt.

While visiting HM Dockyard where these three great memorials of naval heritage are, you may also see a modern link with the Armada. It has long been the custom of the Royal Navy to perpetuate favourite ship names, not all necessarily famous ones. Thus the *Victory* that wore Nelson's flag at Trafalgar was the seventh navy ship of that name. As well as acquiring the name of a predecessor, ships also inherit her battle honours, a generations-old tradition only made official by an Admiralty Fleet Order in 1954; so HMS *Victory*'s roll begins with 'Armada 1588', the first of sixteen actions at which the seven *Victorys* were present. The first *Victory*, an 800 ton ship of 32 guns, built in 1562 and originally called *Great Christopher*, was commanded by Hawkins. The custom applies just as much to modern ships and the nuclear submarine HMS *Dreadnought*, twelfth of her name, is one of half a dozen currently in commission with Armada honours. HMS *Ark Royal*, the Royal Navy's newest aircraft carrier, which you may be fortunate enough to see in Portsmouth, bears the name of Howard's flagship (called the *Ark Raleigh* until Sir Walter sold her to the Crown). Her battle honours board carries the names of actions from the Armada to the Malta Convoys of 1941, when the third *Ark Royal* was torpedoed.

Portsmouth owed its importance initially to its position opposite the Isle of Wight, which was always vulnerable to surprise attacks from across the Channel. Henry had strengthened the town with Southsea Castle, a wooden structure which bore no relation to the surviving later building. He witnessed the loss of the *Mary Rose* from it but he, and Elizabeth after him, preferred to stay and enjoy the hawking at the grander Porchester Castle at the head of one of the harbour's muddy creeks. The Romans built Porchester and it is an imposing edifice still, well worth the half-mile (.8km) diversion from the A27 between Fareham and Portsmouth.

When Wednesday, July 24th dawned, those manning these

defences must have been quite sure that this was the day of reckoning, that the Spaniards must be intending to land the 19,000 troops from the ships on the Isle of Wight, which would give them a secure base from which to replenish before an assault on the mainland in conjunction with the Duke of Parma's even larger army in the Netherlands. Whether Medina Sidonia had now been persuaded that this was the best tactic is open to argument, though it is difficult to account for the course he steered unless it was so. King Philip, making plans on paper in his palace months before, had preferred Margate, so it is easy to claim that was what the Duke was aiming for.

Because of its vulnerable position the Isle of Wight had long had a more complex warning system than the mainland, but it is surprisingly light on fortifications with Carisbrooke Castle, more or less in the centre, the only remaining pile of any significance; so its ultimate defence in the event of a landing relied on the Hampshire levies being shipped over the 2 or 3 miles (3 to 5km) of intervening water. It is fair to assume that on that Wednesday morning Spithead was thick with small vessels carrying men and messages as the red crosses on the bellying Spanish sails became plain and the smoke rose from the island's numerous beacons.

From the hill above the prominent chalk stacs called the Needles (the hill now named Tennyson Down after the Victorian poet laureate who lived nearby), the Armada could be seen coming head on, making to pass the southern shore of the island and about 3 miles (5km) off. This was expected because no large sailing ships used the shallow passage of the Hurst Narrows into the Solent and the invaders were expected to double back into St Helen's Roads in the eastern entrance. They were in sight along the whole coast of the island, right to the southernmost tip and, just as our imaginary walker along the South West Coastal Path has been afforded several grandstand views of the action, so the Isle of Wight provides its own coast path for what proved to be the dramatic finale of the first half.

The path from Freshwater Bay traverses some 15 miles (24km) of cliff scenery, some of them through the Undercliff where prehistoric falls, now covered with woodland, provide a contrasting landscape. The A3055 road which follows the same route a little distance inland also enjoys a commanding seaward view and is quite likely the track from which official observation of the Armada's movements was kept, because the modern road is built along the line of what was known as the Military Road, a patrol route for lookouts in succeeding centuries. As road and path come to St Catherine's Point the modern lighthouse stands on the right, but to the left on St Catherine's Hill stands a far older structure, a thick 6ft (2m) high tower in which monks were known to have burned a light for the safety of ships since 1328. No light shone for friend or foe in 1588, because the Dissolution had put an end to this good work, but it is quite likely that the tower was taken over as one of the beacon sites for which it would be well suited.

All was quiet as the two fleets slowly approached St Catherine's in light airs towards nightfall. There had been no more than a sporadic attack on the Spanish rearguard all day, for the very good reason of Howard's anxiety about his ammunition supplies. He expected that at any moment he would have to engage in one desperate bid to foil a landing and would be scraping his barrels for the last ounce of powder, so he called a council of war which decided on a surprise night attack with a couple of dozen expendable small ships (and presumably expendable men), which could penetrate into the heart of the Spanish formation. This plan was never executed because the night was without a breath of wind, so three hundred ships which should have been in bloody conflict drifted helplessly beneath the cliffs of the Isle of Wight in brilliant moonlight.

First light brought a little wind and the procession moved eastwards until it was off Dunnose Head, 1½ miles (2.4km) beyond Ventnor. What followed is difficult to sort out in detail with any certainty. Once fighting was joined Elizabethan commanders-in-chief could do little to influence events for lack of any effective system of communication and individual captains did not keep minute by minute log books as later generations of sea fighters. Accounts are sparsely worded and limited by the observer's range of vision from his own deck. But broadly the pattern of events on Thursday was similar to that off Portland, with Howard appearing to have disposed his forces rather more efficiently and perhaps having learned something from Drake's probable intervention.

This time there were four squadrons with himself in the centre, Hawkins on his right and Drake on the seaward flank. Again Frobisher held the inshore station and again worked close under the land to gain the windward side of the enemy, an even more important move than before because he was trying now to put himself between the Spanish ships and the entrance to the Solent. On this occasion Medina Sidonia lost no time in sending off his oared galleasses, but this time against Howard in the *Ark* and there was a sharp exchange in which three of them were damaged. Hawkins meantime had engaged some Spanish stragglers and was now hard pressed by other enemy ships that had turned back to their aid. Howard joined this fray and, on the other side, so did the duke himself in the *San Martin*. A general engagement was developing with a heavy expenditure of shot, which Howard knew he could not long sustain. Meanwhile the wind was freshening and moving into the south, leaving Frobisher again cut off to leeward of the Spaniards, just as at Portland. A contingent of Spaniards went bearing down upon the *Triumph*, sure that at last they could board and capture, for she had eleven boats out towing her painfully up wind in a bid to avert the trap. Luckily the wind freshened enough for the *Triumph* and her companions to cut loose their boats and beat out unscathed, leaving the enemy again surprised at the agility of the English ships. Then just as before at Portland, Drake's squadron, reinforced this time by Hawkins, drove down with the now south-westerly wind on the Armada's weather flank, cutting it off from the rest of the fleet and causing great confusion because it was being driven towards the Owers Banks off Selsey Bill, the Sussex headland beyond the Island.

The main Spanish fleet led by the flagship turned from their attempt to reach the Solent and their rearguard action with Howard and sailed to relieve their splintered force. Drake and Hawkins hauled their wind and withdrew seawards before tacking back to rejoin the English fleet. There was no point in them engaging the whole Armada alone and already their move had achieved its object. The Spanish were now to leeward of the island and unable to beat back to the Solent without finding the main English fleet in their way. Already Medina Sidonia had fired the cannon which signalled his ships to resume formation on an easterly course, comfortable in the knowledge that he had no direct orders to establish a base on the Isle of Wight and that by and large his great force was still intact to join up with Parma's army of forty thousand men.

Howard's blessings were mixed ones, too. Another possible enemy landing place was safely passed. He had lost no ships and few men, only one captain having been killed by an unlucky ball. On the other hand his powder barrels and shot lockers were all but empty and the only reinforcements he could rely on were twenty-three small ships, none over 150 tons, left under Lord Henry Seymour to guard the Narrow Seas and the approaches to the Thames. Already he had sent by fast pinnaces for all the powder and ball that could be found in the *Rosario* and *San Salvador*, but the expenditure under Portland and Wight had been great and he would be almost helpless when next the Armada stood to fight.

The solution came from a dozen small ports strung along the south coast. All through the fighting the movements of the English ships had been hampered by hosts of small vessels emerging out of every harbour. Some were regular privateers used to the business of fighting but not to team work, others were just adventurers hoping for the chance to pounce on some small, disabled Spanish auxilliary left astern, or just pick up useful flotsam if one sank. Some were determined to be in the scrap from the best of motives, but they were unorganised and confounded the already intense confusion of the scene. Now Howard put them to use as ammunition carriers so that supplies demanded from the forts and castles along the coast were ferried out by small craft from Newhaven, Winchelsea and Rye and all along the Hampshire and Sussex coast. Throughout Friday men strained at their oars to replenish the fighting ships, which were fortuitously ghosting along in the lightest of airs keeping tail on the Spanish force as it moved towards the French coast. Three hundred and fifty years later more than one writer was struck by the comparison with the little ships that left the same ports in a desperate hour and went to Dunkirk. These little ships solved Howard's chronic ammunition problem, at least temporarily. The men who manned the guns were bothered by another shortage. There was only three days' food left.

7

HILLTOPS ABLAZE

Till Belvoir's lordly terraces the sign to Lincoln sent
And Lincoln sped the message oe'r the wide Vale of Trent,
Till Skiddaw saw the fire that burned on Gaunt's embattled pile
And the red glare on Skiddaw roused the burghers of Carlisle.

('The Spanish Armada' by Lord Macaulay)

Hardly any book written about the Armada in the last 150 years, and there have been dozens, has failed to include a line or two from the poem quoted at the head of this chapter. It was so familiar to earlier generations that writers often didn't bother to mention the source — the Whig politician and man of letters Charles Babington Macaulay whose life spanned the first half of the nineteenth century. Lord Macaulay, as he later became, is notable as the first man to make history popular reading and his works, both prose and verse, enjoyed a wide following well into this century. From 'The Spanish Armada' it is easy to see why. Though it may be out of tune with modern taste, both poetically and politically, it nonetheless paints a vivid word picture of the way England was roused by the warning beacons and does it with a fine sense of pace, the tension mounting stanza by stanza. But did the signals really flare from hilltop to hilltop the length and breadth of the land exactly in the way he describes? How far Macaulay's account is fact and how far poetic fancy is something to examine.

After the engagement off the Isle of Wight the Armada's course towards Calais took it out of sight of the English coast and there was a lull in the fighting, so it is an opportune point for us to leave the coastal scene and follow events inland, discovering what relics of Armada Britain remain to be found. As the beacon signals covered every part of the country, from Land's End to the Scottish border and from Wales to the Wash, a continuous trail following Armada events such as we have followed so far is an impractical proposition, but in every locality there is something to be discovered and readers may enjoy identifying the sites for themselves, even if only with an Ordnance Survey map by the fire.

Hilltop signalling had been known since ancient times. The Greeks, Persians and Romans all used it in some form or another and some of the systems were quite advanced. For instance there is one description of five poles set up on each side of a fire and raised or lowered in a variety of permutations to convey different messages. The Romans don't appear to have brought this advanced use of beacons to Britain, but with a large standing army occupying a small island they probably didn't need it. The first beacons in Britain of which there is any record were on Fair Isle and the Orkneys in AD 943 when those places were ruled by Norway, and they were lit in different places to indicate the direction from which an unfriendly force was supposed to be coming. The first English record of their use was in 1324 when thirty-one beacon sites in the Isle of Wight were mentioned, but the emergency obviously passed because in the following year Edward the Second ordered the number to be reduced, no doubt because they were costing money to maintain. By 1429 the northern counties were also well covered, the danger from the Scots being just as great as that from the Continent. In fact it was not only against a foreign incursion that beacons were useful, because in 1539 they were fired when Henry the Eighth was suppressing a rebellion in the north of England.

By the time Elizabeth came to the throne the system had been developing for 250 years and had reached a high degree of efficiency, so much so that the French ambassador had lately reported home that 'no foreign vessel can show itself without the whole country being roused', while another diplomat estimated that with their warning system the English could move 25,000 to 30,000 men to oppose a landing at any point on the coast within two hours. Elizabeth reviewed all the arrangements within a few months of coming to the throne and through the intensifying cold war of the first thirty years of her reign the orders were frequently revised, so that by 1588 the beacons were part of an organisation that set in train a well rehearsed pattern of events.

The hundreds of stations which covered the country did not just pass a simple alarm from one to the other by means of a single bonfire. Fires were arranged in groups of three, whose pattern of lighting told the next station what action needed to be taken. A search for the sites of these stations does not always take us to the highest hills. Sometimes a smaller isolated prominence offered a better line of sight and in the flat eastern counties braziers on church towers had to serve instead. The iron braziers or cressets used for this purpose survived until recently at Monken Hadley in Hertfordshire and at St Giles, Norwich. On the hilltop sites a standard pattern was usually followed, consisting of a tall baulk of timber set into the ground with a fire-basket suspended at the top and a crude wooden ladder from which it could be lit and fuelled, though in rocky and treeless upland areas a stone structure was probably more convenient. None of the wooden structures has recognisably survived, but in some places the mound on which they were erected is identifiable, as is the case at Lowestoft in Suffolk.

Though there is little hardware to be found, a large number of the sites are identifiable because the purpose for which our ancestors used them has given them a place on the map forever. Anyone can discover their local bit of Armada Britain by plotting and walking the beacon sites found on the Ordnance Survey map. Even the small scale 1:250,000 series reveals a few on every sheet, while the 1:50,000 series enables a thorough search to be made of an area. Many of the spots are marked 'Beacon' in Gothic lettering, but more frequently the history is embodied in the place-name and few sheets do not have their sprinkling of Beacon Hill, Beacon Field, Beacon Point, and so forth. Quite a few are named more fully as Fire Beacon Hill, but others are less obviously named. In Elizabethan times the stations were also commonly referred to as watch houses, or ward posts, so place names on high ground containing 'watch' or 'ward' might reveal an ancient beacon site. So too almost certainly will Telegraph Hill of which there are many in the southern counties, because when the semaphore system was invented during the Napoleonic Wars, enabling the Admiralty to send a simple message to Portsmouth in two minutes on a clear day, many of the old beacon sites made ideal places for the towers of the new-fangled Admiralty Telegraph.

Not all these places are now on open land with a right of way to them, as cultivation, afforestation and urbanisation may have altered the face of the landscape; but a great many remain unscathed in accessible open country and since by definition they are all good vantage points they afford an opportunity for a pleasurable investigation of local history. Many of them seem lonely spots still and must have seemed even more so then to the men who had to guard them. A regular watch was maintained at least in the maritime counties through most of Elizabeth's reign, day and night in the summer months when attack was most likely and in daylight hours only during the winter. Constant watch was sometimes ordered beyond the end of October and even remote inland Leicestershire watched for eighty-two days continuously before the Armada.

Every parish with a beacon had to find four men for a watch so that two were always on duty, but three on duty at a time was specified for sensitive areas like the Isle of Wight. The pay was 8d a day, found by the churchwardens who had to raise the money from a levy on the local population, ranging from 6d for those with an income of £5 a year to 10s for peers and wealthy landowners. The watch were provided with a shelter, but as these were usually wooden structures practically nothing survives. The granite watch house at Wendron in Cornwall, described in Chapter 3, is a rare and possibly unique exception.[*]

* See ref. to Frank Nichol's preserved Beacon Watch House at Shute Hill, Devon (on back fly leaf of this book) (see p. 40).

Care was taken to see that these shelters were not too comfortable. The instructions issued in Kent, for instance, specify that watch houses must be 'without any seat or place of ease lest they fall asleep'. The men were not allowed to have a dog with them either as it might be a distraction. In case all these provisions were not enough to keep the watch alert, inspectors called 'scoutmasters' were employed to carry out spot checks. It was obviously necessary in some places. At Stanway in Essex the scoutmaster found the post deserted and the watchmen off poaching partridges in a nearby cornfield.

The spartan watch house had slits facing towards the neighbouring link in the beacon chain which had to be kept under observation. Outside at some distance from each other stood three separate fire points on their high poles, with supplies of fuel protected from the weather and charges of fat and pitch. Coastal stations set off the train of events by firing one, two or three beacons according to the size and disposition of any fleet of potentially hostile sail sighted. The next station inland did not just repeat this signal to the next up country, but might have to fire a different number according to the circumstances. The purpose was twofold — to pass on the alert to the next county and to summon their own local militia. The number of beacons lighted would determine where the county mustered and whether it would move to the coast, move to a standby position in a neighbouring county or be held in reserve on its own ground.

Urgent though the situation might be, the watchmen themselves had no authority to fire the warnings. Theoretically the overall plan could set 300,000 men on the march (who once mustered had to be paid), so it is not surprising that there were safeguards. An illiterate watchman might well have found it difficult to remember a set of instructions whose drafting would have done credit to any modern official government circular:

> . . . the burnyng but one of them upon the said hilles or upon either of them shall be taken but for warning to the sea coasts in the shire

next adjoyneng to call said help to them without fyering of beacons. And burnyng two beacons together of the three standing upon one of the said hilles shall be warning to the shires next adjoyneng to fyere one of theire two beacons, which single beacon if fyered shall warne all the beacons of Hampshire, Wiltshire, Dorset and Sussex to fyere a single beacon to call all these shires together with speed. And burnynge all three beacons together upon one of the said two hilles or upon both shall be warnynge to the shires next adjoynenge to fyere two beacons to call Oxfordshire, Gloucestershire, Barkshire and Somersetshire to the place appointed to ayde the other shires. And if any nombre of straunge shippes draw to the sea coast in sight without fyer made in the Isle of Wight then to burn the single beacons where the said shippes shall be seen to draw unto and the other two shires next adjoyneng to that coast may burne theire beacons to warne the Isle of Wight to repair to the coaste to theire place appointed. And if so greate a fleet of straunge shippes shall fortunte to be dyscryed and seen to draw to the coasts without any fyer made in the Isle of Wight, so as the number of them shall be deemed to stronge for the shire to defende then to fyer two beacons where the shippes shall be seen as the other shires may do the like to make repaire to the place appoointed.

Even if they could read they might well have been confused by that, so the watchmen's orders were that one of them should go for the constable (an elected part-time parish official in those days) who would in turn find the local justice of the peace who would decide what order to give about the firing of the beacon. Ensuring the correct response was not the only reason for these precautions. For decades before the Armada a jittery country had suffered from false alarms when the militia had been called out unnecessarily. Sir Richard Long complained to the Duke of Suffolk in 1545 that he had needlessly roused all Kent because neighbouring Sussex had sent 'a great alarm that Frenchmen were on the coast', and there were many other instances of trouble caused by pranks and malicious lightings. Hunters smoking out a badger sett on Portsdown Hill in 1579 had half the Hampshire militia marching towards the coast before the mistake was discovered, and several cases are recorded of beacons being fired as a form of protest to draw attention to some injustice. On one occasion there was a plot to light all the beacons round Winchester as a diversion to cover a Catholic rising. Therefore as a precaution against 'the country being troubled with void alarms' as the official orders put it, the magistrates had to send confirmation in writing to neighbouring districts after they had given the word for their own watchmen to light. This went by post, which in those days meant by messenger on foot or horseback and one of each had to be always available.

Fuelling the beacon in the right way was another local responsibility. Wood made leaping flames which could be seen long distances at night, but smoke was better by day. Light-coloured smoke which probably called for large quantities of wet straw was best on bright days; but black smoke achieved by adding animal fat showed up more on overcast ones. About 14 miles (22km) was the maximum range expected. The expertise is not entirely lost. At the Hereford School of Survival and similar places where they teach you how to stay alive in wild places, the art of beacon making in the old way is part of the curriculum, against the day when the rescue helicopter appears on the horizon.

The whole system was kept in existence, even if rather neglected, long after the Armada and the practice of lighting fires on the traditional beacon sites is not dead. They are now lighted at times of national celebration such as the Queen's Silver Jubilee and the marriage of the Prince of Wales. On the former occasion the job of organising the fires and checking up on the old sites was given to the Royal Institute of Chartered Surveyors who plotted the intervisibility of all the points. They made use of about one hundred sites, a fraction of the number on standby in Armada year when Devon alone had over fifty and neighbouring Dorset thirty.

When the beacons blazed in July 1588 it was no mere rabble that answered the call. For the first time in English history they brought out a really organised citizen army, men who knew where they had to go and what they had to do, and that was Queen Elizabeth's achievement. The call to arms of every able-bodied man was a principle as old as the Saxon 'fyrd' which later, under the Normans, became embodied into the feudal system whereby nobles held their land 'of the king' in return for their ability to field an army from their followers, peasants and tenantry whenever called upon. Henry the Eighth set about changing this system because with the passage of time it had kept too much military capacity in the hands of a few powerful families who might not always be loyal to the king. Henry appointed a Lord Lieutenant in every county responsible directly to central government and with the duty of organising a militia of every fit man between 16 and 60.

The militia were to be mustered at intervals, with justices and local gentry serving as officers and with each man responsible for providing weapons suitable to his status. A rich landowner was expected to supply horses, enough armour for a troop of men and a quantity of weapons, while at the other end of a scale which set out a varied shopping list to choose from, an artisan could be called on for a musket, a coat of plate mail or a steel helmet. Other equipment was purchased by the county, especially corslets which were the standard issue armour for foot troops and protected the top half of the body. These were all stored centrally, usually in the vestry or some other room attached to the parish church which was the natural rallying point. Most have long since vanished, but just off the main Ipswich to Norwich road at Mendlesham, near Stowmarket in Suffolk, the village armour is waiting in case the call should come again. It is carefully kept where the villagers returned it when they came home after mustering for the Armada emergency, in the armoury above the vestry in the parish church. The present incumbent, the Reverend P. D. Gray, wisely keeps the armoury locked because other items of value have been stolen from the church in recent years, but it is occasionally opened to public view in summer when someone can be in attendance.

In peacetime the militia was mustered and its arms and weapons inspected about once every three years, but two or three times a year in time of war. Elizabeth the First introduced two new concepts — selection and training. All men between 16 and 60, excepting the nobility and the clergy, continued to be liable for service, but after 1570 only the fit and able were mustered and they were required to undergo regular drill and kit inspections. Henceforward only they were to be called out at a first emergency, the remainder being kept as a kind of Home Guard for a last ditch defence of their own county. This reduced the theoretical 300,000 strength of the militia by more than half. Hopefully it was going to provide more skilful, better disciplined and more effective fighting units.

One reason for this change of thinking was the development of firearms. For centuries all Englishmen had been required to practise regularly with bow and arrow at the local butts (modern street names in many towns still marking the place). To fire off a 4ft (1.2m) long musket, held on a forked rest and to the accompaniment of a loud explosion, was an entirely new experience calling for considerably more instruction and exercise. Special musters for training were ordered in addition to the general ones and those selected became known as the 'trained bands', consisting of musketeers and pikemen.

By and large these obligations were not unpopular with the men as it often amounted to a holiday from a monotonous labouring life and they were paid for it at 8d a day. Some of their employers didn't share this view. The Herefordshire justices complained that no good would come of such goings on and that it would make the men idle and unfit for work, despite the fact that busy times on the land were avoided when calling musters. The lower classes were not slow to complain either when the arrangements didn't suit them and the Elizabethan militiamen don't fit into the popular picture of a forelock clutching peasantry. Firearms training was popular enough for it must have made the younger men, like the ten selected by Hull for drill with the harquebus, seem something like hi-tech heroes to the local girls, but exception was often taken to serving under captains who were not their own local leaders.

They did not like having to report long distances from home either. A march of 10 to 20 miles (16 to 32km) was quite common, but the Sheffield trained bands kicked up a fuss when they were ordered to muster at Doncaster, 18 miles (29km) away. It was not so much a matter of distance as of local pride, and chartered boroughs often demanded the right to make their own arrangements independent of the county.

Another common complaint was having to march in armour, with the result that this was often piled onto carts to follow behind, which led to it being dented and damaged. At their destination the men all rushed to dress for the part and, as one observer wrote, 'whereof little men doo put on great or tall mens armore, and leave little mens armors unfit for great men to put on'. This grievance about marching in armour was so common that in the end the government ordered extra payment for men required to walk more than 6 miles (9.6km) with it on. The city of Bath was more sympathetic towards its brave menfolk and sent them off to fight with woollen linings to their helmets, an expense they certainly would not have contemplated at Oxford whose corporation bemoaned having to forgo the annual civic dinner two years running to pay their share of defending the realm from the Spanish invaders.

The first necessity at a general muster was kit inspection to make sure each man had the equipment he was legally obliged to supply and that the county or the town had provided its quota. This often involved two gatherings, the second after an interval of two or three days when any deficiencies noted had been put right, a proceeding which has left its relic in the English language in the phrase 'to pass muster'. Only then would the lord lieutenant or his deputy make a return, which acted as an authorisation for the men to be paid for their service and gave Whitehall statistics about the strength of forces available.

The inspecting officers needed a sharp eye though. It was at first the practice to call a muster in adjoining hundreds or divisions at a day or two's interval so that the lieutenants could journey from one to the other, until it was found, particularly in Lancashire and Cheshire, that after one area was mustered it was lending all its gear to the neighbouring area so that it too could 'pass muster' without the expense of purchasing all the equipment. To overcome this deceipt, musters had to be called for the same day throughout the region and presumably more deputies employed for the inspection of them. Armour, particularly corslets costing £1 13s 4d a time, seem to have been a particular source of trouble because there were many reports of it being rusty and pitted with holes. However it was noted that Sheffield turned out in well kept armour which it maintained by scouring with sand, oiling and burnishing. Obviously 'Shiny Sheff' was a byword long before there was an HMS *Sheffield* to bear the nickname. Eventually the rest of the country was ordered to appoint armourers who were to be paid 8d per item per annum, to keep the local collection up to scratch.

Armour apart, a good deal of pride was beginning to attach to the local militia and some had uniforms. In Norwich the aldermen clubbed together to deck the men out in green and white and provided tasselled banners. Nottingham sent them all out in ribbons, while Bath had its men's coats trimmed with lace. St Albans went overboard and laid on a feast for its trained bands with a menu that included boiled veal, bacon, roast beef, fresh salmon, sherry and claret and in many places prodigious quantities of beer were dispensed at public expense.

A carnival atmosphere attended many of the musters with the local population turning out to see the sight. In Bristol in 1571 it was reported that there was 'parading with drums and colours and warlike weapons' all of which made 'a comely show'. Serious training was done, nevertheless, and various orders issued from time to time about the drill to be learned. Apart from practising with their weapons the bands were to learn to march in three ranks, take up positions to advance, resist a cavalry charge or defend a post and be familiar with the different drum rolls which were the chief means of communicating orders to the ranks. During the 1580s all this was usually in the charge of an itinerant professional officer and might last three or four days. As the emergency drew closer local commanders were frequently calling extra drills on their own initiative and longer camps were encouraged. Essex got together with Hertfordshire for a joint sixteen-day camp and one or two places organised mock battles, but the county usually kept a very strict eye on the expenditure of powder and victuals for these exercises.

So exactly what happened when the beacons flared and how did these trained bands which were the backbone of the nation's defence on land, react to the call? There was certainly a very clear plan as to how they were to be deployed, but because events were settled at sea and no landing took place, insufficient evidence remains to provide a clear overall picture. This has led some modern writers to question whether the traditional drama of the blazing beacons mustering the militia ever happened at all, but it clearly did in large part, albeit with a good deal of the muddle and confusion that attends all wars. The master plan drawn up in London divided the country into three divisions. One was the militia of the northern counties who were to defend the north-east coast if necessary, but above all to guard the border against the very real possibility of Scotland opening up a second front if the Spaniards landed in the south. A second was assigned to the defence of London and the third consisted of the maritime counties and their neighbours in the south. The latter were expected to be the front line and the trained bands of these counties, and only the trained bands, were to oppose a landing.

No one left a contemporary first-hand description of the scene, but from accounts surviving for supplies of food and hire of carts we know that the western counties did march according to plan as the beacons fired, Cornwall and Devon sending men eastwards as the danger shifted from their shores. We know that when the Hampshire beacons fired the Dorset companies marched towards Portsmouth, because the Earl of Sussex who was in charge of coastal defences there was annoyed to find that there were five hundred fewer than the three thousand he was expecting. In Kent one half of the county's force was drawn up on the coast between Margate and Deal with the other half standing by at Canterbury.

The plan was that the trained bands would harass and delay an enemy landing, falling back as necessary to defensive positions that could be held until the main English army with its stiffening of professional companies, held near London under the Earl of Leicester, could engage in battle. The defence of London was naturally a prime concern and from all points of the compass county troops were converging on the capital while the Armada sailed up Channel. On Tuesday, July 23rd, when the fleets were fighting off Portland, an order was given from London for 20,000 men of the shires to mobilise. This was four days after the *Golden Hind* had sailed into Plymouth with news of the first sighting.

Whether they were summoned by messenger or had already mustered at the call of the beacons and were standing by is not crystal clear, but it seems a reasonable assumption that the fires galvanised the counties of the south and west into immediate action while simply alerting those inland and that this was as it should have been. It would certainly fit in with the Queen's policy, which often looks on examination like one of minimum response. With her throne and nation in jeopardy all her advisers, including Leicester in command of the land forces, urged total mobilisation. Whether she was extremely foolish or extremely cool, or supremely confident in the ability of the navy, can be argued, but she was certainly cunning. Some of the counties were ordered in effect to set off, but not to hurry. While the amateur soldiers travelled, their counties fed and paid them, but once in London the cost fell on the royal purse. So the companies of Northamptonshire were brought up quickly, some covering 60 miles (96km) to London in three days and some in only two, after insisting that the armour should follow behind in carts. But no speed was urged upon Gloucestershire whose companies spent several days at

Cirencester sorting out disputes about weapons and substitutes and was still en route when orders to halt arrived on August 3rd.

Little of all this was of course known in the ranks. As far as they were concerned they had left home to fight a deadly foe. Many of them had been told that the Spaniards were coming with halters to string them up and branding irons to torture their families, as Sir Henry Cromwell reminded his men in Huntingdonshire when he urged them to strict obedience and a godly life. As these men marched across the countryside they must have looked anxiously at the ripening corn. The previous year's crop had been very poor, with wheat so scarce it had fetched three times its normal price in some towns. Now this eventful year looked like producing an abundant crop, but would any of them return home to harvest it?

8

THE QUEEN IN HER HIVE

Our Queen was then at Tilbury,
What could you more desire-a,
For whose sweet sake
Sir Francis Drake
Did set them all on fire-a.

(Contemporary ballad)

The excitement which coursed through the shires as the militiamen made for their village armouries and gathering points was not matched by any dramatic events at sea after the fighting off the Isle of Wight. A two-day lull in the fighting followed as the Spanish fleet ghosted before what little wind there was towards Cap Griz Nez and the English followed ever so slightly out of range. Both sides were now playing a game of bluff. Despite the hundreds of little ships which brought out all the shot and powder that could be found, even robbing the shore batteries and stuffing broken-up iron ploughshares into leather bags for makeshift cannon balls, Howard knew that he had scarcely ammunition enough for a showdown. His policy of keeping the enemy on the move had prevented a landing on the south coast, but the great Armada was still intact for an attempt elsewhere.

Medina Sidonia too was worried about empty lockers. He had plenty of powder, but the expenditure of shot on an enemy that used its agile ships to keep up a game of long bowls was greater than had been reckoned for. Ever since Monday, off Portland, he had been sending fast pinnaces to Parma asking for supplies of shot, but the response was negative. Even more

128

worrying was the lack of reply to his inquiries about Parma's plans for embarking his troops for England, which was the whole reason the duke was there with the greatest fleet of war-ships ever assembled. Though he had come within sight of his objective with no serious losses, time for decision was running out. Ahead lay the North Sea and the shallows of the Dutch coast where his deep-draughted vessels could not be risked and the English gadflies were still on his tail. So in Calais Roads, off the neutral but friendly French coast, he brought his ships to anchor and waited anxiously for news that Parma's army was ready at Dunkirk (then in Flanders) 30 miles (48km) further along the coast.

Almost as if it had been a well-rehearsed drill the English followed suit, and so on Saturday evening and all through Sunday the two fleets watched each other, the nearest within culverin shot, but the flanks 15 miles (24km) and more apart. It is difficult to guess what the Spanish commander in chief thought to achieve by anchoring, for a ship at anchor is not in the best position for fighting. If he hoped that Howard's ships might be swept to leeward of him he was soon disillusioned for they were anchored up wind and, more alarmingly, they soon received unsuspected reinforcements. The squadron of twenty-three small ships under Lord Henry Seymour, which had been left to guard the approaches to the Thames, now came out and joined with Howard. Medina Sidonia was not comforted by a reply from the Duke of Parma that he hoped to have his troops ready for embarkation in another six days, an estimate which the messenger who had seen the state of preparation thought highly optimistic.

Knowing nothing of these difficulties the citizens of London now thought they were a first target for attack. As the Armada had made no effort to land in the west, or take the Isle of Wight, a landing near the mouth of the Thames, possibly at Margate, with a quick march on the capital was deduced to be the Spanish plan. Indeed this was just the strategy recom-mended by King Philip and Medina Sidonia was incapable of considering alternatives, however favourably they might offer themselves. Therefore, four hundred years afterwards London and its surrounding areas are as rich in relics of the great Armada as anywhere else. Before going in search of them it is worth halting on the way at Reigate in Surrey, where a tomb in the parish church enfolds the Lord Admiral of England, Charles, Lord Howard of Effingham, who was laid to rest there thirty-six years after banishing the Spaniards from the Channel. He was eighty-eight and the last survivor of all the leading Armada figures in either country.

For the purpose of this armchair journey the approach to London is best made as the homecoming royal ships would have made it, following the River Thames and turning into its tributary the River Medway on whose banks the naval dockyards had been established.

In Chatham's busy modern High Street stands the most moving of all the memorials the Armada has left behind, the Sir John Hawkins Hospital, built by the man who had been responsible for building the ships, out of compassion for the common sailors who manned them. As we have seen, the English fleet had put to sea short of rations, supplied with bad beer and with sickness rife. After the final encounter it pursued the Spanish fleet up the North Sea as far as the Firth of Forth until starvation and disease forced a return, even though dangerous collusion with Scotland was still on the cards. Beating back down a gale-lashed North Sea there were hardly enough fit hands to work many of the ships and men were dying in their dozens. With no food or other necessities for them captains had no choice but to anchor in the Downs, the open roadstead off the coast of Kent, to put the sick ashore. Boatwork was difficult in the terrible weather, but thousands were landed and left to fend for themselves. They lay in the streets of Margate, Deal and Dover dying of hunger and dysentery.

Howard wrote to the queen's secretary Walsingham on August 29th as urgently as he had pleaded for ammunition a month before:

130

It were too pitiful to have men starve after such a service. Therefore I had rather open the Queen's Majestey's purse somewhat than that they should be in that extremity; for we are to look to have more of these services; and if men should not be cared for better than to let them starve and die miserably we should very hardly get men to serve.

There is no surviving evidence of a royal response, but Howard and Hawkins dipped into their own pockets to relieve some of the distress and the sight of these men dying in the gutters of the Kent ports stirred Hawkins so much, hard-bitten fighter, voyager and slave trader though he was, that he built and endowed a hospital (the word was used then in the sense of almshouses) for destitute seamen. The Sir John Hawkins Hospital still provides a haven for aged mariners and their dependants. Queen Elizabeth the Second visited it recently after interior modernisation had been carried out to provide more twentieth-century amenities behind the sixteenth-century exterior.

That was not all Hawkins did. Together with Sir Francis Drake he started the insurance fund which became known as the Chatham Chest, 'for the perpetual relief of such mariners, shipwrights and seafaring men as by reason of hurts or maim received in the service are driven to great distress and want'. The scheme, novel for the time, was for every man to have a contribution deducted from his pay and because banks were not yet in common use the money was actually kept in a huge chest at Chatham, after which the fund came to be called. Generation after generation of seamen benefited from the Chatham Chest, until 1802 when, after inquiries into irregularities, its funds were incorporated into those of the Greenwich Hospital, home of the naval equivalent of the army's better known Chelsea Pensioners. The chest itself survives at Greenwich where it can be seen in the National Maritime Museum.

This superb museum houses many other exhibits essential to a proper study of the Armada — paintings, contemporary engravings, early charts, navigation instruments and books of the period — and as this book was being written the museum's staff were assembling a major exhibition to run from March to October 1988 to mark the four-hundredth anniversary. But even if the National Maritime Museum were not there, Greenwich would still be an important calling place on the Armada trail. This was Queen Elizabeth's birthplace, her favourite royal residence and the place where she finally signed the orders to resist Spain with force. The present building occupied by the museum, often said to be the most beautifully housed in the world, is mainly later Stuart, but a royal palace has stood on the site since 1427. Elizabeth delighted to watch her ships pass up and down the Thames and see them fire a salute in her honour at the start or finish of some important voyage, as Martin Frobisher did when he set out in search of the North West Passage in 1576 and as Drake did when he went to Greenwich to receive the Queen on board to knight him and have dinner after his voyage round the world. Heavy lorries now thunder between the palace and the river bank, but in Elizabeth's day the lawns ran in gentle slopes down to the water's edge.

The best way to picture what it was like is to climb the hill as far as the Royal Observatory, built by Charles the Second, and look down across the park to the palace buildings. From here the foreshortened view cuts out the traffic and there is an extensive panorama over the river with the masts and yards of the preserved nineteenth-century tea clipper *Cutty Sark* adding to the scenic effect on the left. If you choose your spot carefully you can sit on the Prime Meridian with one foot in the eastern and the other in the western hemisphere. Behind will be Shooters Hill where the last of the Kent beacons roused the Essex shore.

What might have been another stop on the journey into London is now no more than the faintest of echoes. At Deptford, Drake's *Golden Hind* was placed in permanent dry dock after the royal visit at Greenwich and the curious flocked to see her. Their entrance money continued to benefit a sailors' charity for many years until the hull rotted away. The site is now covered in, but some timbers were made into a chair which can be seen at the Bodleian Library at Oxford.

Two other London museums hold Armada relics which are worth seeing. In the British Museum there are about a dozen medals, but I found these rather disappointing, having imagined them to have been rewards for bravery pinned by the queen on the breasts of her sea officers. Instead they are mainly mementos made on the orders of various notable people for private distribution. In fact many of them came from Holland, which had as much cause for rejoicing at the outcome as England, since King Philip hoped that one of the by-products of the expedition would be to complete his subjugation of the Low Countries. The English government had for a long time been supporting the resistance movement there with troops and money, while the part played by the Dutch raiders known as the Sea Beggars in preventing Parma keeping his appointment with the Armada may not have received as much attention from historians as it deserves.

Far more exciting than the medals is the Armada Jewel in the Victoria and Albert Museum. This is a double pendant of enamelled gold set with rubies. The upper circlet about 2¾in (70mm) deep has an unflattering portrait of the queen, her huge ruff finely tooled in gold, while the reverse shows her much younger. The lower part, about 1½in (37mm) deep, has a ship on one side and the Tudor rose on the other. It is thoughtfully displayed under a magnifier so that visitors can fully appreciate the superb craftsmanship of its maker Nicholas Hilliard, born in Exeter and noted as the first English miniaturist, who had his workshop in Gutter Lane off Cheapside. The jewel was presented by Elizabeth to Sir Thomas Heneage, a long serving and favourite courtier who was believed at one time to have rivalled Leicester in the queen's affections and who had the exacting job of being in charge of her war finances.

The puzzle is that this is the only traceable memento of the national victory given by the queen. It remained in the Heneage family until 1902 and was acquired by the V & A for £2,835 when it came up for auction at Christie's in 1935. If there had been other such presentations, they would surely also have been guarded as family heirlooms through many generations and have survived somewhere. There is no record of any other specific honours or rewards following the victory. Hawkins, Frobisher, Lord Thomas Howard and the three lesser known captains had after the engagement off the Isle of Wight been knighted by the Lord Admiral who was authorised to use the royal prerogative, but Howard himself received no recognition until he was elevated to the earldom of Nottingham many years later. Perhaps Elizabeth thought her admirals had already done well enough out of prize money and this is certainly true in the case of Drake. He is estimated to have netted £8,000 from the *Rosario* alone, money he used to buy a fine London house called The Herbery in Dowgate. There is no trace of it today but it was probably in what is now Dowgate Hill, near Cannon Street station.

Nearby, however, a much less known leader has left an unusual reminder of his part in the invasion scare. Just off Bishopsgate in one of those peaceful corners that are sometimes unexpectedly found where London's bustle is thickest, is the church of St Helen's, the resting place of Martin Bond, a merchant adventurer and member of the Haberdashers Company. He was thirty in 1588 and was made chief captain of the London trained bands, a job he obviously did conscientiously for he had 6,000 men drilling twice a week from May onwards. In July he marched at their head to Tilbury and had his moment of glory when the queen inspected the troops there, a moment recorded for posterity on his memorial in St Helen's which depicts in bas relief Bond dressed in armour, sitting in his tent at Tilbury, his horse held ready outside by a groom and with two sentries holding matchlocks.

Although it was to St Paul's, not far away, that Elizabeth went in state four months after it was all over, to lead the nation in thanksgiving, a visit there is not much help on this quest for the building in which she knelt was devoured by the Great Fire of London and replaced by Wren's famous domed edifice.

134

Westminster Abbey is more rewarding for there is her tomb, and Howard too has a memorial although he is buried at Reigate. The Queen's London home at this time was at St James's, the Palace of Westminster having been gutted by fire in the previous reign, not for the last time in its history, but her preference when not at Greenwich was to be up river at Richmond. She spent the Christmas after the Armada there amid much rejoicing.

Moving again downstream, the greatest hive of activity was centred at the Tower, then as for centuries before and after the nation's arsenal. In every age it has housed great stores of arms and armour and today it is the best place to see a wide collection of the weapons and acoutrements used by Elizabeth's defenders. As soon as the Armada was known to be in the eastern Channel however, preparations were focused further down river at Tilbury on the Essex shore where the Thames begins to swell into an estuary for the last 24 miles (38km) of its journey to the sea.

Tilbury has a long history as a strategic position. The Romans built a fort there on the hill at West Tilbury whose ditches and ramparts can still be seen, while the very substantial Tilbury Fort commanding Gravesend Reach from the river bank served over several centuries. It was near the Roman camp that Robert Dudley, Earl of Leicester, tardily appointed 'Lieutenant and Captain General of the Queen's Armies' on the very day the Armada was sighted, began to dig entrenchments in the last week of July.

The half-mile (.8km) width of the river at this point was being blocked by a great boom, the brainchild of the Italian inventor Giambelli. It was made of 120 ships' masts bound with 9in (228mm) circumference rope and held in place by forty anchors, but though it cost over £2,000 it never held together properly and Leicester doubted if it would stop determined ships with a flood tide under them. He was also having difficulty getting sufficient lighters for a boat bridge in case he had to ferry his troops across to Gravesend, but these were the least of the problems besetting the earl. He was supposed to have 23,000 men at Tilbury, made up of the London and surrounding county trained bands, with a stiffening of regular veterans who had served with him in the Low Countries. Another 23,000 were supposed to be deployed near the capital under Lord Hunsdon to guard the queen's person, and the reserves left in the city were preparing for a last ditch fight in the streets.

Leicester worried on the one hand that the county contingents would not arrive in time and on the other that when they did arrive he couldn't feed them. Four thousand armed men, who had mustered at Chelmsford, arrived after a 20 mile (32km) march with not so much as a loaf of bread between them and he marvelled that they didn't mutiny. Foraging parties sent round the district to tempt suppliers with ready money found little response because there was nothing left and eventually Leicester had to send messages to some of the companies to halt where they were and not proceed until they could bring their own provisions with them. On top of this there were difficulties with nobility raising their own forces as of old (it often interfered with the militia arrangements, but confusingly the old legal rights and duties were still not altogether swept away), he quarrelled with his immediate subordinates who disliked his prickly character, and the fact that there was a delay in signing his commission undermined his authority.

It is typical of Dudley's tempestuous career that out of this mêlée of confusion and hasty improvisation he should create one of the golden moments of history. He played the trump card of his long, if chequered, close personal relationship with the queen and asked her to make a personal visit to her soldiers at Tilbury. He of all men could appreciate the magnetic effect of Queen Bess on an English crowd and he alone saw that this was the one thing that could turn a hungry army of unseasoned amateurs into a fighting force with the will to resist. For the queen's part she needed no second bidding, because an even bolder plan was in her own mind. She had already proposed, to the consternation of her counsellors, that she should go to

Dover and place herself at the head of the defences there as a grand gesture of defiance. Leicester snatched at this and turned it to his own advantage by suggesting a visit to Tilbury as an alternative, and the Privy Council reluctantly acquiesced at the less hazardous alternative.

So on August 8th, Queen Bess boarded her state barge with its gilded cabin and was borne down the river by forty oarsmen while a band on board entertained her. When she stepped ashore at Tilbury Blockhouse, where the fort now stands, at noon, a salute of guns rent the air and bands played as she was driven to the camp in a lavishly painted coach which sparkled as if set with jewels, a thousand horsemen preceding her and another thousand following behind. The ranks who could see no more than a glimpse of her at that stage kept up a continual shout of 'God Save the Queen', but it was not planned that she should do more on that day than meet the chief officers.

Although it should be one of the hallowed pieces of English ground not so much as a plaque marks the spot, though it has only recently been positively identified by local historians and this may now be remedied. One man who has been responsible for much of the detective work is Randal Bingley, Curator of the Thurrock Museum Service, who has measured out the ground, comparing the landscape with old maps and prints. There are two places involved, both near West Tilbury village. One where Leicester and the other officers had their tents was at Gun Hill on land largely altered by later quarrying. The troops were assembled on a flat hilltop half a mile away (.8km) along the lanes and a quarter of a mile (.4km) north of West Tilbury church. It commands a good lookout down towards the Thames Estuary in the direction an attack was most expected. It is, as Mr Bingley remarked, a symbolic setting that would have appealed to the theatrical Tudor mind. The land is at present under cultivation.

Ardern Hall, a mile (1.6km) from the camp, 'a proper, sweet, cleanly house', had been arranged for the queen's lodging and from there she returned to the latter camp next morning

137

for what was obviously a superbly stage managed occasion. First the queen, to use a phrase only coined for the second Elizabeth, 'went walkabout', parading up and down the lines on foot with a soldierly gait. Then she reappeared on a splendid white charger which had been a present from Burghley, her Lord High Treasurer, and which had presumably been shipped from London together with the coach.

The impact of her appearance was dramatic. Over her dress she wore a soldier's corslet of polished steel, from which her full sleeves and voluminous skirts billowed out and she went bareheaded. In a gesture of trust and togetherness with her people she had dismissed all her retinue. There were no accustomed guards, no security men. Only a page and Leicester attended her, he also bareheaded and on foot leading her horse by the bridle. After riding round the camp so that all could gain a good view of her, she rode up a grassy mound and addressed the troops. Few beyond the first few ranks could have heard much, but the feeling of the occasion got through to them all:

> My loving people, we have been persuaded by some that are careful for our safety, to take heed how we commit ourselves to armed multitudes, for fear of treachery. But I assure you I do not desire to live to distrust my faithful and loving people. Let tyrants fear. I have always so behaved myself that, under God, I have place my chiefest strength and safeguard in the loyal hearts and good will of my subjects; and therefore I am come amongst you, at this time, not for my recreation and disport, but being resolved in the midst and heat of battle, to live or die amongst you all, and to lay down for my God and for my kingdom and for my people, my honour and my blood, even in the dust. I know I have the body of a weak and feeble woman, but I have the heart and stomach of a king, and of a king of England too, and think foul scorn that Parma or Spain, or any prince of Europe should dare to invade the borders of my realm; to which, rather than any dishonour shall grow by me, I myself will take up arms, I myself will be your general, judge and rewarder.

There was more in which she commended Leicester's leadership and hinted that there would be no difficulties about pay, and the troops cheered themselves hoarse. It was Gloriana at her most glorious, one of the great orations of history, to stand alongside the Gettysburg address or Churchill's 'finest hour' speech. Unfortunately it was also a great anticlimax. By the time it was made the great Armada had already been scattered.

Off Calais on Sunday, July 28th, a rumour had been spread through the Spanish ships, deliberately from the top, that they were anchored because the Duke of Parma was ready to ferry his troops across to England the next day. In fact he was nowhere near an embarkation point and anyway had hardly any flat-bottomed barges, or flyboats as they were called, for transporting troops. The only reason the Spanish fleet was anchored was that its commander did not know what else to do. The English were anchored because they could only wait and see, but that night they broke the deadlock — they attacked with fireships.

Drake is often credited with thinking of fireships, but they were already a well known device. King Philip had foreseen their use and urged his captains to be on their guard against them, while Howard already had several being fitted out at Dover where large stocks of pitch and faggots to charge them had been assembled. What Drake may be credited with is pressing Howard not to wait for these to arrive, but to act at once while conditions were favourable, by sacrificing eight of the smaller vessels already with the fleet. He volunteered one which he owned, the 200 ton *Thomas* and Hawkins offered his *Bark David* of 150 tons. These and six others were stuffed full of combustible material at high speed, without even waiting to remove stores and guns. Hand picked men steered them towards the enemy as the fuses burned, trusting to make a last minute escape by boat.

To sixteenth-century sailors fireships were 'devil ships', regarded like early submarines as an inhumanitarian form of warfare. The sight of a line of eight blazing masses bearing down on the crowded Spanish anchorage just after midnight created widespread panic. Not one of the fireships actually fouled and burned a Spanish ship, but the threat was enough. Almost every ship cut its cables and fled. In the darkness and confusion the Duke showed the leadership that was always to the fore in the face of danger but sadly lacking round the council table and managed to regroup his squadrons in some sort of order around the *San Martin*, but that tight fighting formation that had proved so hard to penetrate was now broken at last.

The chief victim of the night was the *San Lorenzo*, flagship of the galleasses, which collided with another ship in the haste to get under way, damaged her rudder and was wrecked on the Calais shore. When daylight came Howard, with his whole squadron, wasted valuable time pursuing this already crippled ship, but the professional sea commanders saw that this was their chance, probably the only chance, of a successful initiative while the enemy was in disarray. Drake, Hawkins, Frobisher and Seymour, in that order, pitched their squadrons into the disordered Spaniards, while Howard quickly realised his mistake and followed suit. This time there was no playing at long bowls, sniping at long range to keep the enemy on the move. Off Gravelines they closed the range and making every one of their precious supplies of shot tell, gave the Armada a hammering from which it never recovered. At least three crack galleons were sunk, many more ended the day dismasted, leaking or disabled, some with more than half their crews dead. Not a single English ship was lost and the death toll was not reckoned above one junior captain and a hundred men for the whole campaign.

The next morning, Tuesday, another peril faced the Spanish ships when a gale put them on the lee shore of the shoal strewn Dutch coast. Some of their big ships drew 25 or 30ft (7 to 9m) of water and the leadsmen were calling rapidly decreasing depths of water with every heave of the lead. The English stood off to let nature do their work for them while they shared out the last pounds of powder and remaining shot. The Duke of Medina Sidonia had already sent for his priest to absolve him in preparation for the end, when a merciful shift of wind enabled them to sail clear. Once there was safe sea room he called a hurried council of war which decided, that while honour demanded that they should return to the Channel and do battle again, they were in no fit state to do so yet and it would be best to set a course northward. They never did return. The holy mission had failed.

News of all this, or at least the gist of it, was brought to Queen Elizabeth as she was dining in the Earl of Leicester's tent at Gun Hill where, after her triumphant morning with the troops, she was stoutly maintaining her determination to stay with the army. The first messages were confused and, at first it was thought that Parma's army was crossing the Straits without the Spanish navy's help and the queen could not be persuaded to go home. When it became clear that the immediate invasion threat was lifted and the Armada no longer an effective fighting unit, there was no particular sense of elation. For a long time nobody seems to have grasped the significance or the scale of the English navy's achievement. Next morning the queen returned in her barge and Leicester began the job of demobilisation.

Back in London a twenty-four year old actor, who had come to town a couple of years before to try his fortune in Mr Burbage's new theatre at Blackfriars, was thinking of writing a play or two himself when the company got on its feet with the popular revivals they were now doing. What a pity that William never thought of finding a plot in the drama that had just gone on all round him.

9

SCOTLAND'S SUNKEN TREASURE

He made the wynds and waters rise
To scatter all myne enemyes.

(From verses written by Queen Elizabeth the First and sung at the
Thanksgiving Service at St Paul's)

The pursuit of the crippled Armada up the North Sea offered
none of the clifftop spectacle we found travelling along the
south coast, the dangeous off-lying banks dictating a course
well out of sight of land, but the eastern counties did have their
own share of invasion fever.

Harwich probably had details of the English victory before
anywhere else, because Hawkins put in there with a squadron
of thirty-eight ships on August 8th (while Elizabeth was still at
Tilbury) after the pursuit northwards had been abandoned.
Stress of weather coupled with the condition of his fever-ridden
crews drove him in because there was no other reason to use the
Essex port. It had been considered for a naval base but though
Howard himself had visited Harwich early in Armada year and
written: 'It is a place to be made much of for its haven hath not
its fellow in all respects in the realm', it never was developed by
the navy as a permanent base. Further up the River Orwell,
Ipswich had sent 'three sufficient and serviceable hoys' each
with 40 men, including the *William* 140 tons and the *Katharine*
125 tons, while among other Essex ports Colchester sent
another *William* of 100 tons and little Maldon the 186 ton
Edward. If this seems surprising for a port so tiny and mud
bound, the contribution of Aldeburgh up the coast in Suffolk
— the *Greyhound, Jonas* and *Fortune* with a total of 90 hands —

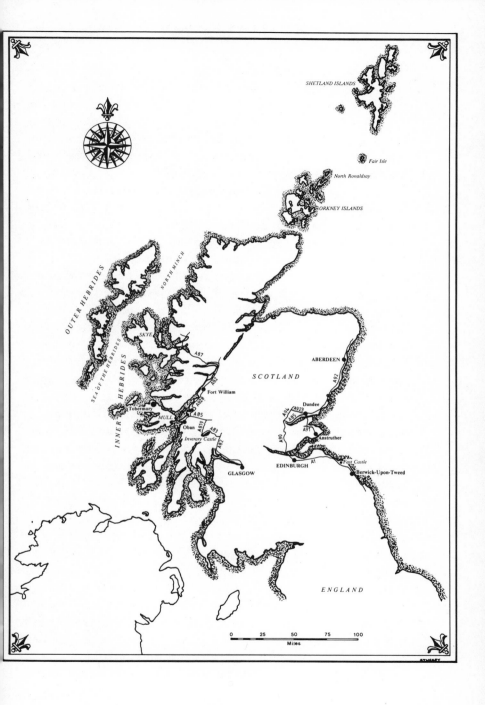

SHETLAND ISLANDS

Fair Isle

North Ronaldsay

ORKNEY ISLANDS

OUTER HEBRIDES

NORTH MINCH

SKYE

SEA OF THE HEBRIDES

INNER HEBRIDES

A87

A82

Fort William

Tobermory

MULL

A85

Oban

A819

A83

Inverary Castle

A83

GLASGOW

SCOTLAND

ABERDEEN

A92

Dundee

A914

A923

A85

A90

A91

Anstruther

EDINBURGH

A1

Fast Castle

Berwick-Upon-Tweed

ENGLAND

0   25   50   75   100

Miles

seems even more remarkable today.

At least the twisting mouth of the Alde provided some sort of haven, but Lowestoft further north still had at that time nothing but an exposed beach. It did not acquire a proper harbour until the middle of the nineteenth century when a short cut was dug from the sea to the stretch of water called Lake Lothing, which sounds remarkably like somewhere out of *Pilgrim's Progress*. Despite this disadvantage Lowestoft supplied two ships, one of which played a significant role. Of the *Gift of God* we know nothing, but the 90 ton *Elizabeth* was the smallest of the eight vessels used in the fireship attack at Calais. Her owner, Thomas Meldrum, received compensation of £411 10s for her loss and claimed another £416 10s for the gear and stores that went up in flames with her. His inventory listed everything he claimed down to four dozen candles at 14s 8d.

Lowestoft can also boast the most easterly of all the English beacon sites. It was raised on a mound of stones which is still there, close to the present lighthouse and just inside the entrance to Belle Vue Park, easily identified because it now has a huge iron anchor resting on it. The steep gorge, known as a 'score' in this part of the world, which runs from there down to the sea leads to the Denes, the open ground where fishermen dried and mended their nets in the days when the port of Lowestoft was packed with herring drifters. Not far away is Lowestoft Ness, the most easterly point in the British Isles, but unlike the other extremities of the kingdom it is sadly unromantic, a neglected spot found by negotiating the maze of an industrial estate. Far more worth a visit while in this part of the world is the nearby museum at Sparrow's Nest run by the volunteers of the Lowestoft and East Suffolk Maritime Society, where the history of the now much diminished fishing industry is preserved. One much prized section tells the story of the Lowestoft sailing smacks which in the First World War did battle with German U-boats with losses on both sides and how Skipper Tom Crisp of the smack *Nelson* won a posthumous VC in his final encounter — a true son of the men who sailed the

144

Elizabeth and the *Gift of God* down to the Channel in 1588.

While those Lowestoft ships were on their way southwards rumour and suspicion were rife around the marshlands inland, an area known then as Lothingland, roughly the stretch between the popular Broads sailing areas of Breydon Water and Oulton Broad. As in many other parts of the land it was expected that Catholic families would be summarily arrested and incarcerated for the duration as a security against treachery from within. A plan had been drawn up for such a contingency as early as 1584 when commissioners had been sent to the district, which was regarded as strategically important. It was practically an island due to the marshes and rivers around, making it a good place to land and establish a presence and it contained a number of influential recusant landowners. The commisioners made a map showing where they all lived in readiness for a sudden raid, but the orders were never given, because Elizabeth trusted her subjects more than many of her advisers did. Throughout the whole emergency only a few of the more openly hostile Catholics were taken up and held at Wisbech Castle in Lincolnshire, but the contingency plan for Lothingland showing the houses that might have heard a hammering on the door in the early hours has still survived in the Public Record Office where it was interpreted by local historian David Butcher.

One of the reasons for Lothingland's importance was the vulnerable position in which its capture would place Great Yarmouth, just across the River Yare which forms the boundary with Norfolk, especially as there was a long tradition of enmity between the Norfolk port and its Suffolk neighbour Lowestoft over fishing disputes. Not to be outdone by Lowestoft the citizens of Yarmouth fitted out the *Grace* of 150 tons for the Armada campaign. Round the great bulge of Norfolk at King's Lynn they commissioned the *Mayflower*, but complained to London about the difficulty of getting any contribution from Blakeney, Cley or Wells. The parsimony of Wells particularly annoyed the King's Lynn burgesses because it was, they said, 'a town very well furnished with shipping, within which there are many rich men inhabiting'. The most northerly east coast port of which any Armada record survives is Hull where they were having more than just financial difficulties meeting the government's requirements. All the local ships, they pleaded, were away on foreign voyages and as ninety-four local seamen had already been pressed into the navy there were no more left at home.

Beyond the Humber the Armada has left little evidence, but this does not mean that the northern counties were not involved, only that their resources of men and arms were earmarked for defence of the Scottish border in the event of King James throwing in his lot with Spain. Once over the border however, the scent is stronger again and now we are on the treasure trail of Spanish gold. It was off the Firth of Forth that the English fleet turned back and gave up the pursuit, a decision forced as we have seen by hunger and disease. An unsubstantiated report spoke of the Lord Admiral himself having to live off a plateful of beans.

None of the leaders was confident that the Armada could be safely left at that point. The Spaniards might use Scottish neutrality to repair their damage, restock and return down the North Sea (referred to in Spanish accounts as the Norwegian Sea). Drake expressed the opinion in a hurried despatch to the Queen that they would alternatively seek aid from the sympathetic King of Denmark before making a return. The mood of the English seamen was in fact one of despondency, for in their worn out and hungry state they did not realise the extent of the victory they had won. They felt they had only warded off the evil hour because lack of powder, shot and provisions had left them unable to finish the job.

If the Spaniards had wanted to seek aid in Scotland, and there is no proof that they did, they had plenty of money on board the hundred or more ships now running before the southerly gale, to pay or bribe their way and there are those who believe that some of it is cached away in Scotland still. Just before the entrance to the Firth of Forth, near the prominent seamark of St Abb's Head, stands the clifftop ruin of Fast Castle. The story, which keeps re-emerging in different forms, credits one Colonel Sempill, a Spanish secret agent in Scotland, with landing a boatload of gold and silver from one of the Armada ships at a rendezvous in the mouth of the firth and hiding it at the castle. It was evidently not with the connivance of the owner, a man called Robert Logan, because there is an account of him making a frantic search of his own grounds for it only half a dozen years later.

On and off, hopeful diggers have been looking ever since. The evidence for any landing of money or rendezvous of any kind is wafer thin, but hope springs eternal in the treasure hunter's breast. One account, published as late as 1986, has the gold coming from a ship which is supposed to have 'limped ashore at Anstruther', the latter being an attractive fishing port on the opposite shore of the Forth in Fife. Both the ship and her commander are named, but unfortunately there is incontrovertible proof, as we shall see, that both were far to the north on a less hospitable shore. There was a glimmer of hope for the legend in 1969 when excavations uncovered some coins, together with a cannon ball and a few bones, but as the coins bore the heads of Elizabeth the First and James the First they did not lend much weight to the Spanish connection.

By the time he saw he was no longer pursued, the Duke of Medina Sidonia had already made up his mind that the only sensible course of action was to return home northabout round the British Isles and keep as much of his fleet as possible together to fight another day. It still consisted of over a hundred ships, which Scottish fishermen counted passing between North Ronaldsay and Fair Isle on August 10th and heading west. So far they had all kept together, but at this point three ships lost touch with the main body and spent the next twelve days battling against headwinds without making any progress. On the tenth day one of them, the *Barca de Amburg* of 600 tons, foundered and sank, her 25 crew and 239 soldiers all being rescued by her two companions, though they were themselves in a very poor state with gaping holes in their seams. After this the remaining two ran north until a shift of wind to the north east at last enabled them to set course towards Spain. This respite lasted only three days, then the wind blew strongly from the south west and drove them back in the direction they had come, patching their leaks with ox-hides as they went. One of them was the 650 ton *El Gran Grifon*, the ship that hopeful treasure hunters at Fast Castle have coupled with the landing of the Spanish money. She did indeed leave treasure in Scotland, not in the form of gold coin, but objects more valuable for the knowledge they give us of the ships which sailed to restore the true faith to the English heretics. She was also one of the most gallant ships in the Armada.

The *Gran Grifon* came from Rostock and was either chartered or forcibly requisitioned along with a German crew on one of her regular trading runs to Spain. She was an unlikely ship to see much action because she was one of the 'hulks', meaning not as the word does today, a derelict vessel, but a store and supply ship, in other words what we should call a fleet auxiliary. Altogether twenty-three sailed with the Armada and we have already seen the fate of three of them — the *Barca de Amburg* (or *Barque of Hamburg*) recently sunk, the *San Pedro Mayor*, which struggled right round the British Isles and back up the Channel to be wrecked at Hope Cove in Devon and the *San Salvador*, crippled by an internal explosion on the first day's fighting.

All these hulks were organised into one squadron of which the *San Salvador* was what the Spanish called the *almiranta*. This looks as if it ought to translate as 'flagship', but actually means 'vice-flagship'. The flagship was known to the Spanish as the *capitana* and the *capitana* of the squadron was *El Gran Grifon*. On board her in charge of the squadron was a nobleman, Juan Gomez de Medina, a man obviously fitted for a more active command. His orders were to keep his squadron inside the great crescent formation where it would be protected by a screen of fighting ships, rather like merchantmen in a convoy with destroyer escort, but on several occasions the *Gran Grifon* was found among the fighting. Off Portland she was out in the rearguard supporting Recalde. In the battle off the Isle of Wight she was again on the perimeter, where she stood up to broadsides from the *Revenge* which killed seventy men and did extensive damage, until she was towed out of trouble by two galleasses. Nevertheless Gomez de Medina repaired his damage at sea and was in action again at the final engagement off Gravelines. He seems a spirited and resourceful man and he comes out with credit to the end because although he eventually lost his ship, he got most of his men safely home to Spain.

By September 16th the *Gran Grifon* had lost sight of her remaining companion and was back between Orkney and Shetland, a rock-strewn area of fierce tide rips. The pumps were no longer able to contain the inrush of water through the battered hull, so Gomez de Medina decided to beach the ship as soon as he could. He brought her to anchor at the south-eastern tip of Fair Isle, halfway between the main Orkney and Shetland groups. An attempt to beach the ship in a controlled way failed and she ended up being wrecked under cliffs in a narrow gully called Stroms Hellier where she eventually sank, but not before more than three hundred men aboard her had got ashore.

Though they were saved from the wreck their plight was not enviable, for they had no food and the 6 square miles (15km²) of barren island scarcely supported its handful of inhabitants. Fifty of the *Gran Grifon* survivors are believed to have died and the site of their common grave by the shore, marked on the map as Spainnarts Graves, is one of the more desolate relics of the Armada. It speaks volumes for the character of Gomes de Medina that though the population of Fair Isle amounted to a mere seventeen households and could easily have been overwhelmed by the numbers of Spanish soldiers, albeit weary and hungry ones, there was only peaceful negotiation for what little the islanders could spare towards feeding so many unexpected visitors. Some money and valuables had almost certainly been got ashore, but no amount could have bought what did not exist. It was a month before the weather abated sufficiently for a boat to be sent to the Scottish mainland for help and some weeks after that before a ship was found to take the Spaniards off Fair Isle and land them at Anstruther from where, after many more wanderings, they found their way home a year later.

The *Gran Grifon* herself sank out of site in the rocky cove against whose cliffs she had come to rest and only recently some of the 'treasure' has been recovered. The location of the wreck, the piecing together of the story and the raising of a number of cannon, some shot, items of ship's gear and utensils was a remarkable piece of archaeological detective work led by Dr Colin Martin of St Andrews University. It was one of three Armada wrecks which he discovered. The relics found by him and his team on the *Gran Grifon* can be found now in the County Museum at Lerwick, the capital of Shetland, to which Fair Isle administratively belongs.

You do not have to go to either Lerwick or Fair Isle however to see what many believe to be a most unusual legacy of the *capitana* of the Armada hulks. It has been widely held — and just as widely refuted — that some of the traditional patterns of Fair Isle jumpers owe their origins to the wreck on the island of the unfortunate Spanish ship. Some detect in their intricate design Catholic symbols copied from possessions of the castaways, while others ascribe a much older pagan Norse origin to the same devices. Clearly there isn't enough evidence to connect the knitwear which is Fair Isle's chief claim to fame with the Armada, but neither does there seem enough to dismiss the link. The strongest clue is that one of the repeated motifs of traditional Fair Isle looks remarkably like a griffin, the heraldic beast with an eagle's head and a lion's body, and as Dr Martin pointed out *El Gran Grifon* — the *Great Griffin* — came from Rostock whose town arms bore a griffin. The wrecked ship may well have carried a figurehead carved to represent the hometown symbol. If the theory holds good you may well be walking round with your own reminder of the Armada.

Although the location of the *Gran Grifon* had been always approximately known the remains had been undisturbed down the centuries until the sub aqua investigators set to work. Far different is the story of one of her companions which came to grief 200 miles (320km) further south in the Western Isles. This is the wreck which is supposed to hold the fabulous treasure of Tobermory, the search for which has gone on for four hundred years. Kings have intrigued to gain possession of this horde reputed to be worth £30m. Two dukes have died as a result of defending their right to it and in every age down to the present it has attracted cranks and speculators as well as more serious explorers.

Tradition gives this treasure ship the name *Florencia*, but as no vessel of that name appeared in the Armada lists earlier historians decided that she must be the *San Francesco*. Unfortunately all three ships of that name in the fleet were accounted for elsewhere. Later it was established she was probably *San Juan*, but this saint was honoured by even more Spanish ships. The limitations of hagiographic nomenclature make life very difficult for Armada scholars. Only in the last few years has the identity of the Tobermory galleon been fixed beyond reasonable doubt as the *San Juan de Sicilia*, an 800 ton ship of the Levant squadron which carried 63 mariners and 279 soldiers.

To anyone sailing on the west coast of Scotland, or even taking the hydrofoil trip from Fort William, the haven of Tobermory on the island of Mull is a welcome sight with its sheltering arms of hills. The colourful cluster of pleasantly proportioned houses, which give the place a comforting toytown appearance from the sea, were the fruits of a Victorian philanthropic enterprise to foster the local fishing industry and probably only a few black cabins of the type once common to Highland crofts stood there in 1588. Even so the men of the *St John of Sicily*, used to warmer and calmer waters, must have counted themselves lucky to have come safely to such a secure anchorage after being so long battered by Atlantic gales.

Their ship, too, had been badly damaged in the fighting at

Gravelines and they needed time to carry out repairs and stock up with food and water before making another attempt to head home. It must have seemed as if their luck was in when they were offered the help they needed by the local chief Lauchlan Maclean, whose castle at Duart 6 miles (9.6km) to the east is today a visitor attraction and still inhabited by his descendants. However Maclean's price was high. He demanded as payment the services of one hundred of the experienced Spanish soldiers embarked on the *San Juan* to reinforce his clan in raids on rival chiefs on neighbouring islands.

This arrangement the captain of the Spanish ship was in no position to refuse and it detained him in Tobermory Bay for six weeks, well into November, by which time word had spread to the court in Edinburgh and from there via the English embassy to Whitehall, that there was immense wealth on board and all the ship's officers were richly decked in jewels. While both countries were buzzing with speculation the ship was suddenly rent by an explosion which sent her to the bottom. Why it happened has been giving rise to even more speculation ever since. There are numerous theories — Maclean had her treacherously blown up after professing friendship because he couldn't take the treasure from the well armed ship by force, an English spy disguised as a provision merchant hid aboard and lit a fuse, a young Maclean relation given as a hostage against the return of the soldiers decided to cause the explosion and escape. These are all reasons which have been advanced with nothing but folklore to sustain them. It may of course have been a careless accident in the powder room. Whatever the cause of the sinking it was by no means the end of the story.

It chanced under Scottish law that all salvage rights on that coast belonged to the Admiral of the Western Isles, a position held by the chief of the powerful Clan Campbell, the Earl of Argyll; but as soon as news of sinking reached court, King James found an excuse to deprive him of the post (which wasn't difficult as the earl had been living abroad for years) and revert the salvage rights to the Crown. As diving technology then was not even in its infancy the move availed the king little and he was probably too preoccupied afterwards with becoming First of England and Sixth of Scotland to do more about it.

When the ever impecunious Charles the First came to the united throne he sold the rights back to the Argyll family to raise cash, but when the first crude diving bell was invented and given promising trials by the 8th Earl, his successor Charles the Second tried to exploit a loophole in the agreement to nullify the arrangement, whereupon Argyll took the case to court and won. It may or may not have been coincidence that he was later arrested on trumped up charges of treason and beheaded. However even absolute monarchs don't always get things their own way and Charles was prevented from confiscating the Argyll properties and rights. So he sent his brother, the Duke of York, to Scotland to find out what the situation was with regard to the wreck and, on learning that German and Swedish divers had already brought up a number of iron guns for the new earl and might at any time reach the treasure itself, he began afresh to spin a devious web which led to the 9th Earl being framed like his father and sentenced to death. This time the king was a little smarter and connived at the escape of the condemned man from Edinburgh Castle to the Continent, so that he could legally confiscate all his property and privileges as a fugitive.

When the Duke of York came to the throne as James the Second, he began in earnest contracting with engineers who whetted the royal appetite further by recovering twelve guns, this time more valuable brass ones. Meanwhile the fugitive 9th Earl abroad had joined the short-lived Monmouth rebellion and landed at Tobermory to drum up Scottish support, so James was able to execute him on reasonable grounds and remove for good, he thought, any troublesome claims about the Spanish gold. Before King James could get his hands on it, however, William of Orange landed at Brixham and by his side was the 10th Earl of Argyll who was rewarded by the new King William with a step up the peerage to dukedom and the restoration of all possessions, including the right to the wreck which the present

Duke of Argyll continues to enjoy.

This happened exactly one hundred years after the Armada. Since then hardly a decade has gone by without fresh attempts to discover what lies beneath the silt where the *San Juan* went down. Every small advance in diving gear or technique has brought renewed interest and fresh offers to have a go. A glint of gold in the form of a few coins or a plate with signs of armigerous ownership have occasionally rewarded long, arduous and expensive searches; but apart from cannon balls, more guns and minor items of gear that is all. A collection of these is now displayed in the museum at Tobermory devoted to the fascinating story of the four-hundred-year search. There are also guns and other relics from the wreck at Inverary Castle on the mainland, the great seat of the Dukes of Argyll which is open to visitors.

As far as the £30m horde itself is concerned there must be a very big question mark over its existence. Burrowing through the mountains of surviving Spanish documents a Scottish writer, Alison McLeay, has recently pieced together the accounts for the *San Juan de Sicilia* from the period she was chartered in the Mediterranean and through her fitting out in Lisbon until the Armada sailed. In her book *The Tobermory Treasure* which tells the whole story in great detail, she concludes that the ship could only have been carrying the sort of contingency money which all captains had. It is a cogent and entertaining piece of detective work, but it is unlikely to put an end to continuing searches for Spanish gold in Tobermory Bay.

10

THE IRISH GRAVEYARD

We were driven on a sandy beach, surrounded on all sides by great rocks, a most terrible spectacle, and in the space of one hour all the ships were dashed to pieces.

(Letter to King Philip from Captain Francisco de Cuellar, a survivor)

The main body of Spanish ships which safely negotiated the perils of Scottish waters still had a long journey before them and so have we. It stretches along the whole Atlantic facing coast of Ireland, from the strange volcanic rock formation of Giant's Causeway at the north-east tip, right round to the south-western extremity. The fact is that Ireland has more of what remains of the Armada than anywhere in the world, including treasure such as Tobermory only dreamed of, and the reason is that it became the graveyard of King Philip's fleet.

When the remaining hundred or so ships turned westward off the Orkneys, no longer any pretence being made that they might make a fresh attempt, the Duke of Medina Sidonia issued detailed orders about the course they were to follow, being well advised by his pilots of the dangers of the 1,500 mile (2,414km) voyage ahead. It involved making a long board 400 miles (644km) out into the Atlantic as far as Rockall, so that they might then have a fair wind for Spain on a track well clear of all land. He cautioned them to 'take great care lest you fall upon the island of Ireland, for fear of the harm that may befall you upon that coast'.

The *San Martin* herself made port in Spain a fortnight later, whereupon the Duke limped ashore a broken man, pitifully petitioned the king to relieve him of his command and then fled

155

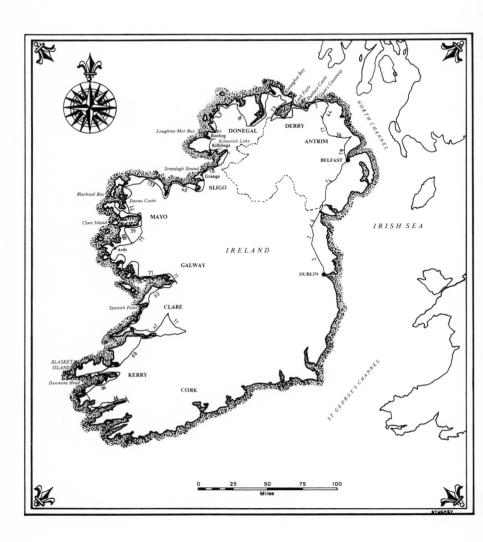

NORTH CHANNEL

Mulaghor Bay
Loch Foyle
Dunluce Castle
Giant's Causeway

Loughros Mor Bay
DONEGAL   DERRY
Rosbeg
Kiloorish Lake   ANTRIM
Killybegs
BELFAST

Streedagh Strand
Grange
SLIGO

Blacksod Bay
Doona Castle   IRISH SEA
Clare Island
MAYO

Ards

GALWAY

Spanish Point   CLARE

BLASKET
ISLANDS   KERRY
Dunmore Head

CORK

IRELAND

DUBLIN

ST GEORGES CHANNEL

0   25   50   75   100
Miles

to his castle at San Lucar in a curtained coach, stoned and booed along the route. Over the next few weeks another sixty-five ships arrived in twos and threes, almost all totally unfit for further use and every one full of sick and dying men. Altogether it is reckoned that only one third of the ships which set out from Lisbon in May came back, but the toll in men was even more appalling. Considerably less than one in three ever saw home again.

Of the estimated 20,000 who died in the campaign as a result of enemy action, sickness or shipwreck about half did so in Ireland, where at least twenty-six of the ships which had followed the *San Martin* round the north of Scotland met their end. There are any number of reasons why so many of the captains did not follow the sailing directions given to them. Many were Mediterranean sailors without experience of the grey Atlantic and whose ships were of a lighter build, unable to stand the buffeting of the ocean rollers. They may have been tempted to take a short-cut course closer to land. Those who had charts probably sealed their doom by trusting them, because early cartographers had given Ireland a much flatter west coast, leaving out the bulge of counties Mayo and Galway, which is where many of the wrecks occurred. There were also some ships with Irishmen aboard. At least forty Irishmen are recorded in the Armada, which is not surprising as the country had a close interest in Spanish success which they hoped would rid them of the English. It is quite likely that their presence held out promise of help from fellow countrymen and shelter from the English occupying authorities if a landfall could be made. Other crews were simply driven onto the Irish coast by stress of weather, unable to work to windward with damaged ships, and others must have sought it out of desperation for food and water. Whatever the reason nearly all those who reached the coast met a terrible end. Those that were not drowned were either killed for their belongings by savage inhabitants, or slaughtered by English troops sent to ferret them out. A few managed to reach home after long and painful wanderings.

157

On no vessel in that northabout voyage can life have been more hell than on the one surviving galleass, *Girona*. Because the galleass was a hybrid between a full-sailed galleon and an oared galley her sailing qualities were never very good and for auxiliary power she relied on three hundred slaves chained in gangs to thirty-two huge oars. It is hard to imagine which was worse for them, the back-breaking strain of rowing for long shifts or the misery of being tossed helplessly about when conditions made rowing impossible. Of all the ships that left Lisbon in the summer the *Girona* seems one of the least likely to have been a treasure ship and she left with no huge chests of king's gold, yet by a strange set of circumstances she has yielded up glittering prizes, the only ship so far to have provided the sort of Spanish Armada treasure around which legends have grown. If we pick up the westward trail in Northern Ireland the *Girona*'s is the first of the wreck sites to be reached.

On her homeward voyage she had originally battled much further to the westward and rounded the corner into Donegal Bay, where she found a sheltered anchorage to lie up. Ashore the crew found the countryside swarming with their fellow countrymen who were either sheltering and foraging like themselves, or who had survived from shipwreck. Among them was a prominent officer, Don Alonso de Leyva, a soldier with a long record of bravery and a personal favourite of Philip's, who carried with him the king's commission to take over as commander-in-chief of the expedition if Medina Sidonia was killed. He had already been shipwrecked twice in northern Ireland in a few days and now, finding a third ship still afloat, he took charge of the situation in the area.

Of the damaged ships in the vicinity de Leyva decided that the *Girona* was the most serviceable, so he had her made as seaworthy as possible by cannibalising others and decided to take in her as many men as she could carry and try to reach neutral Scotland. There were around 2,000 men ashore and on the abandoned ships and about half of them were packed into the galleass, making with her own complement around 1,300 on board. Now such was the reputation of Don Alonso de Leyva that he had a very large personal following consisting of the scions of many of the most wealthy families in Spain, noble adventurers and other young bloods all with their own retainers and these, together with high-born officers, had the priority places in the ship. As it was their custom to carry much wealth on long journeys because it might stand them in good stead in emergencies, all these wealthy voyagers had set out with their own caskets of jewels and gold which they had succeeded in preserving and which went with them now on board the *Girona* when she put to sea again in the last week of October.

Several days later they were only 30 miles (48km) short of clearing the Irish coast en route for Scotland when another storm struck and smashed the *Girona*'s patched up rudder. At midnight she was swept helplessly onto the Antrim shore and ripped out her bottom on the reef by Locada Point, just east of the Giant's Causeway. Of the 1,300 souls on board only 9 reached land. Within minutes the galleass broke into pieces under the pounding of the waves, scattering the chests and money belts of the passengers across a wide area of the sea bed.

This wreck has left its mark in three place names, Port na Spaniagh, Spaniard Rock and Spaniard Cave, a fact which attracted the attention in the 1960s of Robert Steniut, an experienced Belgian underwater archaeologist, not the sort to be carried away by dreams of Spanish gold. One of the first finds he made was an anchor, vainly cast overboard in an attempt to arrest the ship's wild career towards the breakers. Guns and shot and other artefacts of historic interest followed. Only then did he and his team begin to discover, under the deep encrustations of time, heaps of gold coins, silver crosses, jewellery, candlesticks, even rings engraved with parting messages from loved ones. It was then that he began to piece together the story of how so much wealth came to be aboard the lumbering galleass that left Lisbon with an inventory fit only for her complement of soldiers and galley slaves. Altogether Steniut's expedition recovered over 1,000 gold and silver coins, 35 gold jewels, 12 gold rings, 8 gold chains and 2 silver crucifixes together with several thousand nautical and military relics, domestic articles and humbler personal possessions. They are preserved now in their own special Girona Room at the Ulster Museum in Belfast.

The nine survivors of the *Girona* found their way to Dunluce Castle, perched perilously on the overhanging clifftop a dozen miles (20km) along the coast towards Portrush. It has been a fortified site since the thirteenth century with a view from its walls on a fine day as far as the Western Isles of Scotland. At the time of the Armada it was occupied by the chief of the McConnells, a fierce resister of the English who gave shelter to hundreds of survivors from other ships along the north coast. Those who were lucky enough to meet a friendly reception and to escape the searching English troops would naturally have been directed to the dwelling of the chief. McConnell not only sheltered the Spanish but organised escape routes and there is circumstantial evidence that he was well rewarded for his trouble with money or valuables brought ashore, because a year later substantial extension and rebuilding was carried out at Dunluce. Those Armada payments may be the reason so much of it stands in good shape today.

The county of Donegal in the north-east corner of Ireland accounted for eight Spanish ships. The first of these was *La Trinidad Valencera*, 1,100 tons and the fourth largest ship in the Armada, her home waters the Spanish possessions in Sicily. *La Trinidad* had fought a gallant action at Gravelines as one of that rearguard which saved the fleet from total rout. She was the other ship in company with the *Gran Grifin* when the *Barc de Amburg* went down and took off the other half of the survivors. By this time however her own condition was not much better and she was making water fast when she ran into Kinnaghoe Bay at the mouth of Loch Foyle, some 30 miles (48km) north of Londonderry, where she was beached. All but forty of those aboard her got ashore, but the ship herself soon broke up. The remains have been discovered by members of the Derry Sub

Aqua Club and properly excavated under the expert super-vision of Dr Colin Martin. Several bronze guns have been recovered which have provided useful new evidence about the Armada's armament.

Further west at Loughros Mor Bay near Rosbeg lies a wreck which has not excited quite as much attention from divers, but at the time excited quite a number of people in England. This is the *Duquesa Santa Ana*, the ship on which Don Alonso de Leyva embarked after his first shipwreck. Like the *Girona* she was also trying to head back to Scotland and, like the *Trinidad Valencera*, had to be run ashore to prevent her sinking. Though he was already sick or injured de Leyva was an experienced military commander who soon had a disciplined organisation ashore. Either by threat or persuasion he occupied a small, easily defended castle on O'Boyle Island in Kiltoorish Lake, a little way inland, strengthening his position with guns landed from the *Duquesa*. Appreciating the value of intelligence he sent out scouts who eventually discovered the *Girona* and two other Spanish ships in Donegal Bay. Contact was probably also made with other wandering groups of survivors. He then organised a march of a thousand men for 20 miles (32km) through the mountains to the sheltered inlet at Killybegs where the *Girona* was. In the procession were carried all the weapons and valuables stripped from the ship and De Leyva was carried at its head in a litter. They left behind the big guns which the local McSweeney chiefs no doubt thought a reasonable reward for their co-operation. Fragments of their castle wall are still standing.

Even in this remote corner of Ireland the movements did not escape the English intelligence service which was already 'monitoring' Armada ship sightings round the Irish coast. What they learned of the landings from the *Duquesa Santa Ana* and the rendezvous with other ships sent messages of alarm speeding to Sir William Fitzwilliam, the Lord Deputy who governed Ireland from Dublin Castle. Here was a Spanish com-mander marching through British territory with a force of a thousand armed men and enough money to buy local support, which might be all too readily forthcoming. Strung round the coastline were other groups that might join him. The English army in Ireland was small, probably no more than 1,800 men, in line with Queen Elizabeth's policy of never incurring more expenditure than was absolutely necessary. It had to rely on harsh methods rather than numbers to keep the country in submission. There was therefore no knowing what a general of De Leyva's reputation might be able to do. When the news reached London it was enough for the queen to order hurriedly raised reinforcements to be shipped. Just for a time it seemed possible in London that the Spaniards might turn the tables at the eleventh hour and snatch victory from the jaws of defeat.

More immediately orders were given that all prisoners should be put to death, excepting always of course those who could offer a handsome ransom. That policy of wholesesale slaughter, harsh even for the times, was mainly the result of the fear aroused by the energetic leadership of Alonso de Leyva, Knight of Santiago. At Killybegs he eventually embarked in the *Girona* for his third and fatal voyage, but that intention was not clear to the spies who saw his columns marching through the hills of Donegal looking more like an army on the move than a bunch of castaways.

Further south in Sligo three ships which had kept together sought respite off Streedagh Strand, a long stretch of gently curving beach near Grange. They rode at anchor there for four days waiting for a favourable shift of wind, but instead it started to blow violently from the west and all three were dashed upon the rocks. One of those ships was *La Lavia*, the vice-flagship of the Levant squadron which had on board a man doubly fortunate to escape, because he was a prisoner under sentence of death.

Francisco de Cuellar had been captain of the 500 ton galleon *San Pedro* until deprived of his command and given the death sentence for allowing his ship to be off station after Medina Sidonia had issued that stern order to all captains, just after the battle off the Isle of Wight, not to break formation. Another captain was hanged on the spot for the same offence, but de Cuellar had managed to obtain a stay of execution and was now held in custody by the advocate general of the fleet on *La Lavia*. After a series of amazing adventures he reached Antwerp from where he wrote to the king a 10,000 word letter relating all that had happened to him and pleading for his sentence to be quashed. This document has become one of the principal sources of information on the fate of the Spanish in Ireland.

For months after he had seen hundreds of his countrymen's bodies washed up on the shore he lived a Robinson Crusoe existence, having been robbed of everything including his clothes, so that he was thankful in the end to be captured and used as a slave by a local smith. Escaping eventually from this bondage and finding other survivors who had dodged the English pickets, he led them as a band of mercenaries fighting for an insurgent local chief until they were able to earn a passage to Scotland. Anyone who wants to picture what the scene was like on Streedagh Strand on that wild September day could do no better than turn to Captain Cuellar's description:

> . . . in the space of one hour all the ships were dashed to pieces and not three hundred men escaped. More than a thousand were drowned and among them many persons of rank, captains, gentlemen and others. Don Diego [commander of one of the other ships who was known as the hunchback colonel] died more pitifully than ever was seen in this world; for in fear of the boisterous waves that swept over the ship, he took his tender, which had a deck, and he together with the Count of Villafranca's son and two others, Portuguese gentlemen, taking more than sixteen thousand ducats' worth of jewels and crowns, got down below the deck of the tender [ship's boat] and had the hatchway fastened down over them and caulked [sealed]. Then immediately over seventy men who were still alive threw themselves from the ship onto the tender and while that was struggling to make its way to the shore, a great wave came over it, which sunk it and washed off all hands that were on it. And straightway the tender went tossing with the waves hither and thither, until it reached the beach, where it stuck fast upside down, and by this mishap the gentlemen who got under the little deck perished within.

He goes on to describe how 'whenever any of our men reached land, two hundred savages and other enemies stripped them of everything they wore, leaving them stark naked and without any pity beat them and ill used them'. His account of the desolate scene is corroborated by an English report which speaks of 1,100 bodies being counted on a 5 mile (8km) stretch of beach.

The coast of adjoining County Mayo has two notable Armada wrecks. One is *La Rata Coronada*, an 820 ton Levantine which was the ship in which Don Alonso de Leyva originally left Spain and which ran aground at Blacksod Bay. As he did in Donegal, de Leyva got nearly all the men ashore and took up a strong position, this time in Doona Castle, a small section of which is still standing as his monument. Again, as on the second occasion, he reconnoitred and led his men across country to another ship, the *Duquesa Santa Ana*, which we have seen took them back towards Scotland until her own sinking at Loughros Mor Bay. The other Mayo wreck is *El Gran Grin*, *almiranta* of Recalde's Biscay squadron which sank off Clare Island. At least three others of lesser note also went down in the same area.

Galway has Duirling na Spainneach near Ards as a reminder of the fate of another of Recalde's ships, *La Concepcion*, while neighbouring County Clare has its Spanish Point where the *San Marcos* struck a reef when carrying four hundred men. Survivors in this area were unfortunate enough to be handed over to the local English governor, Sir Richard Bingham, whose iron-fist rule had earned him the nickname 'The Flail'. Harbouring the Spanish was punishable by death so the local population could hardly be blamed for their compliance.

Our journey in search of Armada Britain ends where the last act of the drama was played out, on the deeply fissured south-west tip of Ireland. The Land's End of Ireland is Dunmore Head in County Kerry and those ships which clawed their way past it could shape a course for Spain with no further hazards. The great Recalde had brought his flagship the *San Juan* this far by

September 7th. Despite having been more in the thick of the fighting than any other she was in reasonable shape, though some of the ships in company with her were not and Recalde sought shelter to try and help them.

It is a menacing stretch of coast affording little refuge from the Atlantic, rock bound and cloaked in mist more often than not. Two miles (3km) off the headland are the Blasket Islands, a small group of which the largest is Great Blasket, 5 miles (8km) long and rising 900ft (274km) from the sea for most of its length. Fierce tide rips tear through the sound between the island and the mainland, but in desperate circumstances it offered Recalde a slender chance of shelter for the mixed little squadron of stragglers of which he now found himself in charge. In a daring act of seamanship he led the squadron through the narrow channel between the islets and anchored to repair the ships as best he could to survive the rest of the voyage. First however it was essential to find water and if possible food, because they were down to a quarter pound of biscuit a day per man. A boatload of men sent ashore to see what they could find were surprised by an English patrol which had observed the arrival and they never returned. Undaunted, another party filled water casks by scaling the cliffs of Great Blasket and tapping a small spring.

To confuse matters two other ships in company with the *San Juan* at this time were also called *San Juan* being, in full, *San Juan Bautista* or *St John the Baptist*. One of these Recalde made more seaworthy by transferring gear from his own ship, but the other was found to have poor hope of staying afloat so it was decided to transfer her complement to the flagship *San Juan* and two unidentified smaller ships that were also in company. Before this could be accomplished the weather worsened and they were all riding it out in the narrow sound with straining cables when two more Armada stragglers swept in from the north. In attempting to anchor, one of them fouled the cables of Recalde's ship and one of the other *San Juan*, causing them both to drag. Both captains had a frantic struggle to hoist sail to get their vessels under control and managed to anchor again and avoid being swept onto the rocks, but the new ship was not so fortunate. She struck hard and went down so fast that she took all hands with her, except for one man who managed to swim ashore where he was interrogated and shot.

The new ship was the *Santa Maria de la Rosa* the 945 ton *almiranta* of Oquendo's squadron. Her remains were located by divers in 1968 and she has been scientifically investigated, although the archaeologists had trouble in warding off illegal underwater fortune hunters. An anchor, several guns and a set of pewter plates identified by the crest of their owner have been recovered.

Undeterred by this disaster Admiral Recalde continued with his plans to transfer men from the sinking ship and even strip out her guns to take back to Spain, if it could be managed. Eventually on September 8th when the weather had abated they sailed clear and set course for home. Only then did Recalde, who was sixty-two, take to his bunk, worn out by his exertions. As he lay he probably thought how strongly he had advised Philip that unless they first destroyed the English navy no invasion could succeed and how often he had urged Medina Sidonia to take his nose out of the King's long memoranda and go on the offensive. Four days after arriving at Corunna he died without leaving the ship, an embittered and broken-hearted man.

At the start of this journey in search of Armada Britain it was said that it was not the intention to re-examine events which have been analysed by generations of able historians, but it is impossible to end without reaching conclusions of one's own. Even after four hundred years the outcome of the Armada is still being debated and rightly so, because new evidence does come to light, particularly as a result of developments in marine archaeology. In this respect the Armada has more resemblance to the battle of Jutland, a clash of two great armadas of ironclads which still leaves a question mark over who really won, than it does to Trafalgar which left no room for argument. Everybody

166

recognises that many contributory factors played a part, but almost all writers have been tempted to pick out some single cause more decisive than others.

At one time it was fashionable to consider that the weather enabled the English to win and it certainly played havoc in the end, but it was never that bad in the Channel where the wind changed twice in the Spanish favour and again to save them from the Dutch sandbanks. It suited Spanish reports subsequently to exaggerate the wind force and it suited English policy to show that, despite the patronage of Rome, God was on her side. The legend of the little ships against the great galleons has also been put in perspective. Hawkin's new breed were certainly handier and a larger number of smaller vessels made up the English fleet, but a comparison of front-line ships shows them to have been much of a tonnage with the *capitanas* and *almirantas* and in any event they would never have dented that solid Spanish wall had the opposition been really determined, as the pattern of the early encounters shows.

Neither was there anything inferior about the enemy's seamanship, for Spain could hardly have built and maintained an empire in the New World without first-class mariners. Professor Lewis proved in his masterly analysis of the fighting that though English gunnery was more advanced it was still undeveloped and too ineffective at long range to be the deciding factor once thought. More recently the marine archaeologist Sydney Wignall has made a metallurgical study of salvaged cannon balls and concluded that the Spanish navy was duped by dishonest contractors who supplied badly cast shot which seriously hampered their fire power. This enterprising and novel piece of historical research has produced valuable new knowledge, but as the sampling was only a tiny proportion of the 120,000 balls carried by the Armada it is hard to accept as a major factor.

If all these studies into the causes of the Spanish failure have a weakness it is that of being more concerned with materiel than men. What comes over strongly as a result of following its progress round the British Isles is that the great crusade turned into a fiasco mainly because none of its leaders had any stomach for it. The damp air of defeat hung over it from the start. Why else should a great military organiser like Santa Cruz find the preparation so wearisome that it hastened his death? Why else should Medina Sidonia, certainly never the indolent fool he used to be painted, write as if his appointment were a virtual death sentence? Why should courageous old Recalde talk, before they had even set out, of needing a miracle to defeat the English? Above all, what kept the able Duke of Parma from having his army anywhere near ready for embarkation when the ships had been expected for months? The answer can only be that they all felt the whole plan was wrong and all at various times had their diplomatically couched advice ignored by a king too wrapped up in his own thoughts to pay any heed. Bravado was for the noble young bloods who sailed as *aventuros*, but the leaders sailed with heavy hearts and the king's stultifyingly detailed orders. Even the Pope, in whose name it ostensibly all was, had no faith in the plan and refused to part with a penny until Catholic soldiers were actually marching on English soil. The enterprise had become like some great bureaucratic dinosaur staggering under its own weight and all the other factors combined to break its back.

England at the same time was on a rising star of dynamic individual enterprise, the country of the new men whose time had come. What she won by her determination that summer was her place in the front rank of nations and confidence to start building her own empire across the seas of which she now felt mistress.

Looking back on it, this tour of Armada Britain has evoked conflicting moods of patriotism, of amazement at what was accomplished by poor and hungry men of both countries and the selfish response of some of their betters, and occasionally of sheer hilarity at the abiding national genius for muddling through. If that is how it seems, it is no doubt because that is how it was — and how we should have found it if we had made the journey in 1588.

BIBLIOGRAPHY

Information about the Armada campaign and ships
Cuellar, Captain Francisco de. *Letter to His Majesty King Philip II* (Corn-market Press, 1970)
Fallon, Niall. *The Armada in Ireland* (Stanford Maritime, 1978)
Froude, J. A. *The Spanish Story of the Armada* (Longmans, 1892)
Lewis, Michael. *The Spanish Armada* (Batsford, 1960)
Martin, Colin. *Full Fathom Five* (Chatto & Windus, 1975)
Mattingley, Garrett. *The Defeat of the Spanish Armada* (Jonathan Cape, 1969)
McLeay, Alison. *The Tobermory Treasure* (Conway Maritime, 1986)
Navy Records Society. 'Documents Illustrating the History of the Spanish Armada', *Naval Miscellany*, Vol 4 (1952)
Navy Records Society. State Papers Relating to the Defeat of the Spanish Armada (1894)
Society for Nautical Research. *Mariners Mirror*, numerous vols

Biographical information
Froude, J. A. *English Seamen in the 16th Century* (Longmans, 1919)
Jenkins, Elizabeth. *Elizabeth and Leicester* (Gollancz, 1961)
Lewis, Michael. *The Hawkins Dynasty* (Allen & Unwin, 1969)
Mason, A. E. W. *Life of Francis Drake* (Hodder & Stoughton, 1942)
Petrie, Sir Charles. *Philip II of Spain* (Eyre & Spottiswoode, 1963)
Thomson, G. M. *Sir Francis Drake* (Secker & Warburg, 1972)
Wilson, Derek. *The World Encompassed* (Hamish Hamilton, 1977)
Dictionary of National Biography

General historical and military background
Boynton, Lindsay. *The Elizabethan Militia* (Routledge, Kegan Paul 1967)
Dickens, A. G. *The English Reformation* (Batsford, 1964)
Elton, G. R. *The Tudor Constitution* (Cambridge University Press, 1960)
Lewis Michael. *The Navy of Britain* (Allen & Unwin, 1948)
Manning, T. D. and Walker, C. F. *British Warship Names* (Putnam, 1959)
Rowse, A. L. *The Spirit of English History* (Jonathan Cape, 1943)
——. *The Elizabethan Renaissance* (Macmillan, 1971)
Trevelyan, G. M. *History of England* (Longman, 1926)

White, H. T. Unpublished manuscript on fire beacons in Devon County Record Office (Ref 56/16)

Local information
Burton, S. H. *The South Devon Coast* (Werner Laurie, 1954)
——. *The Coasts of Cornwall* (Werner Laurie, 1955)
Capper, D. P. *Moat Defensive (A history of the waters of the Nore Command* (Arthur Baker, 1963)
Dawson, C. M. *The Story of Greenwich* (C. M. Dawson, 1977)
Fielder, Duncan. *History of Bideford* (Phillimore, 1986)
Gill, Crispin. *Plymouth: A New History* (David & Charles, 1979)
Harris. W. Best. *The Lizard Coastline* (W. Best Harris, 1984)
——. *Cremyll to Crafthole* (W. Best Harris, 1983)
Hemery, Eric. *Historic Dart* (David & Charles, 1982)
——. *Walking Dartmoor Waterways* (David & Charles, 1986)
Oppenheim, M. *Maritime History of Devon* (Exeter University Press, 1968)
Devon & Cornwall Notes and Queries — various vols
Transactions of the Devonshire Association — various vols
Western Antiquary — various vols

ACKNOWLEDGEMENTS

I am indebted in the first instance to Dr Stephen Fisher of the Department of Economic History, Exeter University, for drawing my attention to the impending four-hundredth anniversary of the Armada and for help on matters of maritime history on various occasions.

Grateful thanks are also due to the Reverend Stanley Ward for acting as my guide to his native Plymouth. The leading historian of that city, Crispin Gill, was generous with his guidance, in addition to the reliance I placed on his published work. Local historians John Corin and Tony Pawlyn in Cornwall and David Butcher in Suffolk also kindly shared their local knowledge. Mr Randal Bingley, Curator of the Thurrock Museums Department, Essex, freely placed at my disposal the fruits of his own research at Tilbury. Jane and Grant Wilson kindly ferreted out useful information about beacons and on that subject the Ordnance Survey Information Branch and the Royal Institute of Chartered Surveyors were most helpful.

Other institutions whose staffs gave me valuable assistance include the National Maritime Museum at Greenwich and the Coins and Medals Department of the British Museum, Suffolk Records Office and Weymouth Museum. Margaret Bradley of BBC Bristol went to a lot of trouble to track down an elusive quotation. I am also grateful to the commanding officers of HMS *Drake* and HMS *Ark Royal*.

In the course of research I was glad of the excellent facilities of the West Country Studies Library in Exeter, the Naval Studies Library in Plymouth, Devon County Record Office and Exeter University Library.

For any sources of help overlooked I sincerely apologise. Any errors are of course entirely my own and in no way due to anyone mentioned here. Photographs are acknowledged as they appear. Unless otherwise stated they are my own. The maps were all drawn by Peter Stuckey.

INDEX

People

Aragon, Catherine of, 13
Argyll, Dukes of, 152 et seq

Bedford, Dukes of, 58, 83
Bergman, John, Mayor of Poole, 106
Bingham, Richard, 164
Boleyn, Anne, 13
Bond, Martin, 134
Burghley, Lord, 19, 104, 134

Cary, Sir George, 85, 89, 92
Charles the Fifth, Emperor, 13, 16, 18
Churchill, Winston, 10, 81, 139
Clement the Seventh, Pope, 13
Cranmer, Archbishop Thomas, 14
Cromwell, Sir Henry, 127
Cuellar, Capitan Francisco, 162, 163

Drake, Edmund, father of Francis, 83
Drake, Lady Elliott, 58
Drake, Sir Francis – early voyages, 22 et seq; at Cadiz, 25; early life, 51, 52; Plymouth property, 54; game of bowls tradition 56 et seq; graffiti mystery, 61; residence and relics at Buckland Abbey, 63 et seq; builds Drake's leat, 81 et seq; birthplace, 83; captures Rosario, 87 et seq; action off Portland, 102; comparison with Nelson, 107; action off Isle of Wight, 111; concern with seamen's charities, 131, 132; knighted, 132; London properties, 134; part in fireships attack, 139; involved in final engagement, 140.
Drake Thomas, brother of Francis, 64

Edward the Sixth, 16
Elizabeth the First – character and policies, 19 et seq; organisation of militia, 120, 122; fondness for Greeenwich, 132; rewards for Armada service, 133, 134; at Tilbury, 136 et seq; hears news of victory, 141; policies in Ireland, 142

Elizabeth the Second, 62, 131

Fitzwilliam, Sir William, 161
Flemying, Captain Thomas, 56, 99, 104
Frobisher, Sir Martin – foreign voyages, 23, 132; burial place, 61; relations with Drake, 88; action off Portland, 101; action off Isle of Wight, 111; knighted, 134; part in final engagement, 140

Gilbert, Sir Humphrey, 23
Gilbert, Sir John, 90
Gregory the Thirteenth, Pope, 35
Grenville, John, son of Richard, 85
Grenville, Sir Richard, 63, 84

Halliard, Nicholas, jeweller, 133
Hawkins, Sir John – foreign voyages, 21 et seq; in charge of royal dockyards, 48 et seq; in command of Victory, 99, 108, 110; concern for poor seamen, 131, 134; part in final engagement, 139, 140; lands sick crews, 142.
Hawkins, William, 48, 49, 53, 55
Heneage, Sir Thomas, 133
Henry the Eighth – relations with Rome, 12 et seq; sets up navy board, 50; dissolution of monastries, 14 et seq; coastal defences, 102; in Portsmouth area, 107, 108; suppresses northern rebellion, 115; changes militia system, 121.
Howard of Effingham, Admiral Lord – takes command of fleet at Plymouth, 53 et seq; engages enemy off Eddystone, 59; incident off start Point and relations with Drake, 87 et seq; confusion caused by Drake's action, 91; events off Portland Bill, 101 et seq; anxiety about ammunition shortage, 104, 108, 112, 128; action off Isle of Wight, 111 et seq; events off Calais, 129; burial place, 130; knights commanders at sea, 134; uses fireships, 139, 140; at Harwich, 142
Houyghton, James, 90

172

Ships

176

Frank / Sue / Fiona.
Nichols.

(see chapter 7, esp. pp 116-7.).

Forest Properties in Devon;

SHUTE HILL, near SHUTE, AXMINSTER, Devon.

SY 258 974 (Grid Ref. for Shute Hill Armada Beacon.
This beacon (or, rather, beacon keepers hut has been fully restored
circa 1994 and was officially opened by ~~Frank~~ Frank in mid July 1994
in the presence of local dignitaries + children from Shute Primary School.
The children have done research on Parish Records and the like to
find out the history of the Beacon. It appears to have been first
established in the 1560's. The actual beacon would probably have
been in an iron cage supported on a pole alongside the Beacon
keepers hut. The hut would probably be manned from about
March to October in Tudor times - the likelihood of invasion would
not have been great in mid winter. (Frank's other forest property in
Devon is on Heydon Hill, near Withycombe, Wiveliscombe, Devon.
ST 04 27. Frank has also got a Triangulation pillar on ~~his~~ his forest
property at Shute Hill.

The only other preserved stone Beacon in Devon is near Wellington,
near the Wellington monument. ST 13 17. (according to Frank).
But see pages 40-1 for ref. to Beacon Hut on Little Wendron hill (mawhay
Beacon), grid ref., SW 69 30.